DISCOVERING THE SMALLEST CHURCHES IN SCOTLAND

DISCOVERING THE SMALLEST CHURCHES IN SCOTLAND

JOHN KINROSS

The History Press

In the mists of the future lie tremendous possibilities of both triumph and failure. The Church carries with it the destiny of coming generations of our countrymen, and of that beloved and ancient thing, our Scottish fatherland.

John Buchan, *The Kirk in Scotland*, 1930

First published 2010

The History Press
The Mill, Brimscombe Port
Stroud, Gloucestershire, GL5 2QG
www.thehistorypress.co.uk

British Library Cataloguing in Publication Data.
A catalogue record for this book is available from the British Library.

ISBN 978 0 7524 5880 9

Typesetting and origination by The History Press
Printed in Great Britain
Manufacturing managed by Jellyfish Print Solutions Ltd

CONTENTS

THE CHURCHES

LIST OF ILLUSTRATIONS

Monochrome Figures

Colour Plates (between pages 64 & 65)

Front cover: Eriboll Church. Photograph by P. Mitchell FBIPP, AMPA from a painting by Sue Challis

Rear cover: St Oran's Chapel, Iona

All photographs by the author unless marked otherwise.

MAPS

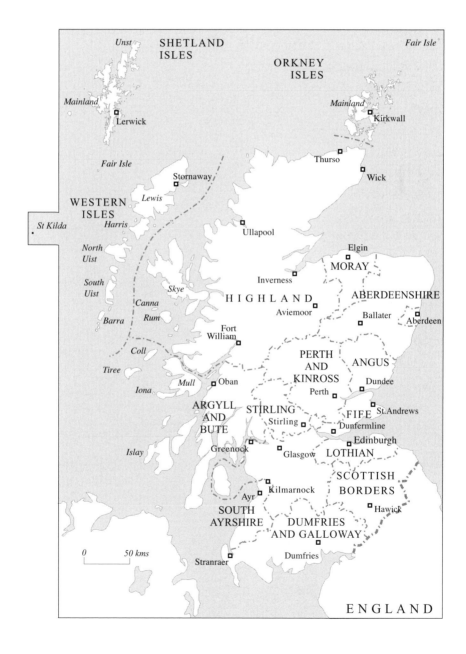

Unst

SHETLAND
ISLES

ORKNEY
ISLES

Fair Isle

Mainland

Lerwick

Mainland

Kirkwall

Thurso

Wick

Fair Isle

Stornaway

WESTERN
ISLES

Lewis

St Kilda

Harris

Ullapool

North
Uist

Elgin

MORAY

South
Uist

Skye

Inverness

Canna

HIGHLAND

ABERDEENSHIRE

Barra

Rum

Aviemoor

Ballater

Aberdeen

Fort
William

Coll

Tiree

PERTH
AND
KINROSS

ANGUS

Iona

Mull

Oban

Dundee

Perth

ARGYLL
AND
BUTE

STIRLING

FIFE

St.Andrews

Stirling

Dunfermline

Islay

Greenock

Glasgow

Edinburgh

LOTHIAN

SCOTTISH
BORDERS

Kilmarnock

Ayr

Hawick

SOUTH
AYRSHIRE

DUMFRIES
AND GALLOWAY

0   50 kms

Stranraer

Dumfries

ENGLAND

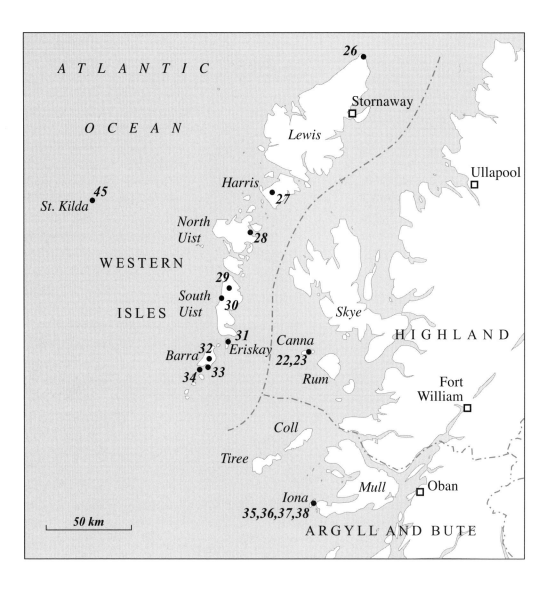

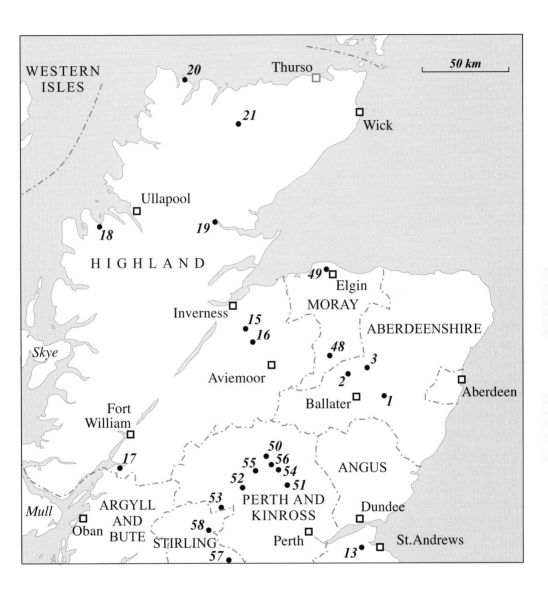

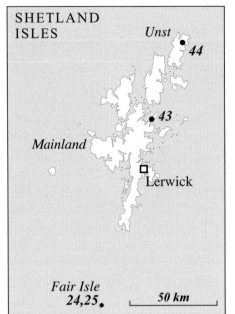

SHETLAND ISLES

Unst
44

43

Mainland

□ Lerwick

Fair Isle
24,25 •

50 km

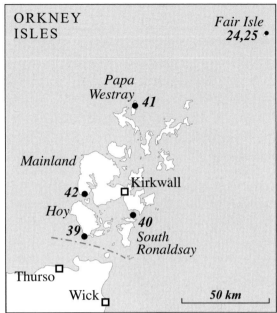

ORKNEY ISLES

Fair Isle
24,25 •

Papa Westray
41

Mainland

42 • □ Kirkwall

Hoy
40
39 • *South Ronaldsay*

Thurso □

Wick □

50 km

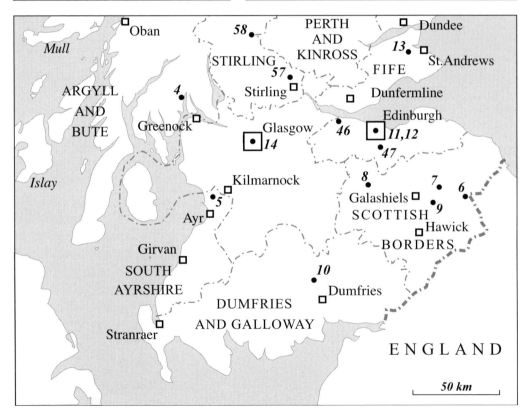

□ Oban

Mull

58 •

PERTH AND KINROSS

□ Dundee

13 • □
St.Andrews

STIRLING

57 •

FIFE

ARGYLL AND BUTE

4 •

Stirling □

□ Dunfermline

Greenock □

Glasgow □
• □ **14**

46 •

Edinburgh
• **11,12**

47 •

Islay

Kilmarnock •

8 •

7 •

6 •

Galashiels □

9 •

SCOTTISH

5 •

Ayr □

BORDERS

□ Hawick

Girvan □

SOUTH AYRSHIRE

10 •

□ Dumfries

DUMFRIES AND GALLOWAY

Stranraer □

E N G L A N D

50 km

FOREWORD

I feel honoured to have been invited to write an introduction to John's latest book, not least because in his previous work he very kindly quoted a paper that I gave at a conference as being one of his sources of inspiration. I feel encouraged, humbled and pleasantly surprised that the words spoken so long ago are not only remembered but have actually provoked further thought and action!

My real sense of gratitude at being asked to do this, however, is because it deals with two areas that have been and remain so important to me. Small churches are frequently ignored or forgotten. The buildings are often humble in origin and design. They are likely to be simple and straightforward and the current congregation small and possibly elderly. Yet the prayer life of that small group of people is frequently deep and far-reaching and their faith and the expression of it frequently profound.

It was in and through such churches that my faith was born and nurtured and it's been my privilege to have ministered to and been ministered by such congregations for the past 40 years. It therefore comes as a delight to find a book and an author that treasure and value both the buildings and the people who worship in them.

To find that the geographical focus of the book concerned is north of the border only adds to the sense of pleasure. My family roots on my mother's side are firmly fixed in the West Highlands and I've always had a great pride in my Scottish heritage, and from my earliest days have always viewed it as home. That is exactly what it now is as I have a house not too far from where my mother was born in Glen Coe. The sense of belonging to a place, an area and a culture is very real and very strong. It has a great deal to do with history and the way that it has been shared and passed on, but it has also had much to do with the faith of the people concerned. The two are inextricably linked and my journey of faith owes as much to them as it does to the churches of which I've been a part.

Hence my sense of gratitude for being invited by John to write this foreword, for God has blessed me through both the small churches and Scottish people who have worshipped in them.

Rev Gordon Gatward
Director, Arthur Rank Centre

ACKNOWLEDGEMENTS

There have been a number of people who have helped me in the research for this book. First of all David and Sheila Walker in Edinburgh, then Tom Davidson Kelly, J.W. Nimmo, Rev Dr Ian Bradley, John Hume for general help, and Norman Marr and Teresa Coomber (in Aberdeenshire) and fellow Reader Donald McKee in Lewis. Thanks again to Alison Poole for her drawings, to John Taylor who drew the maps and to the staff of *Country Way* who helped search out some past articles, and especially to their Director, Rev Gordon Gatward, who has written the above Foreword. Special thanks to Sue Challis for the painting of Eriboll and to Sallyann, once again, for preparing the manuscript.

INTRODUCTION

The Church in Scotland

For those of us brought up in the Church of England it is very difficult to understand that the Church of Scotland is Presbyterian, but the lesser Episcopal Church, which has been going since 1765, still has bishops and is the nearest to the English Church. There is an excellent but lengthy book, J.H.S. Burleigh's *A Church History of Scotland* (OUP, 1960), that explains it all. I have included the author's chart here, which may make it seem more complicated than you the reader expect.

The first Christians in Scotland were supposed to be St Columba and St Ninian. Columba came to Iona from Ireland. Most of his Christians were monks and they settled on islands like Tiree, Mull, Islay, Skye and on the mainland at Kintyre, Morven and possibly Loch Awe. However, in the fifth century St Ninian arrived at Whithorn; by the eleventh century his monastery, known as Candida Casa, had become a bishopric controlled by the Archbishop of York. Aidan in Lindisfarne was sent there at the time of the Synod of Whitby (AD 66) and it was Aidan's successor, Colman, who represented Scotland. In spite of Iona being sacked several times, relics of St Columba reached the church at Dunkeld thanks to the Pictish king, Kenneth MacAlpin.

By the mid-thirteenth century the monasteries had several appropriated churches (Kelso had 37, Holyrood 27, Paisley 29 and Arbroath 33). Even today the Abbot of Pluscarden takes services from time to time at the little church of Our Lady of Perpetual Succour, Chapeltown (see page 89). King David (1124) decided that the premier bishopric in Scotland should be St Andrews with Glasgow as second. By the time he died there were nine Scottish bishops with two Norse ones (Orkney and Sudreys (Sodor) coming under Trondheim). Nowadays the Church of England has a diocese called Sodor and Man. In 1192 Pope Celestine III declared that the Church of Scotland had sees at St Andrews, Dunblane, Glasgow, Dunkeld, Brechin, Aberdeen, Moray, Ross and Caithness. This helped the bishops to argue that they did not come under York. By 1465 St Andrews had become a metropolitan see with an Archbishop, and King James IV elevated Glasgow to the same heights.

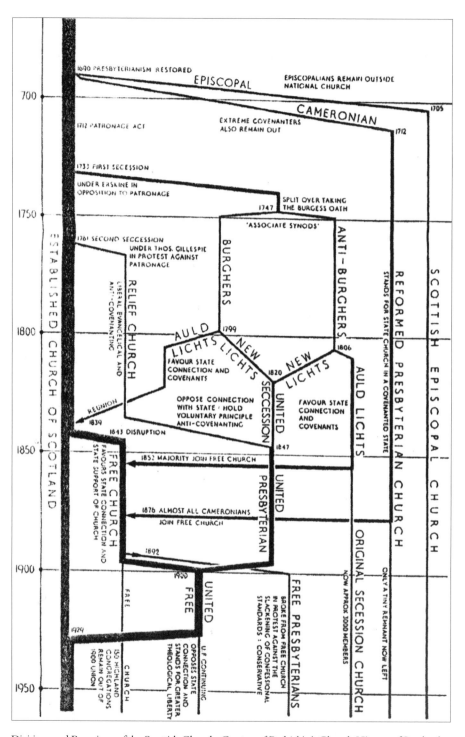

Divisions and Reunions of the Scottish Church. *Courtesy of Burleigh's* A Church History of Scotland

The death of the Archbishop of St Andrews beside his king at Flodden in 1513 gave Pope Leo X an opportunity to put his own nephew up as a candidate for the vacancy. Luckily, Andrew Forman was preferred by the Scots but Papal interference was something that led to the terrible murder of the Archbishop Sharp in 1679 by Hackston of Rathillet and his Covenanters.

The defeat of Charles I and his son, later at Worcester, did not augur well for the Scottish bishops. The Union of England and Scotland in 1705 guaranteed the Scottish Church its independence but it was the Presbyterians, founded by Knox and Melville, that became the Church of Scotland and the Episcopalians who broke away and became the smaller church, as indeed they are today.

Troubles arose with the breach of the Act of Union (1707) when patrons were reintroduced for appointing ministers. In 1733 Ebenezer and Ralph Erskine signed an Act of Secession in protest but their group was divided into Burghers and Anti-Burghers and again into New Lights and Old Lights on a theological point. Most rejoined by the twentieth century and only the Wee Free in the outer isles plus a few others remain; as well, of course, as the Roman Catholics, Quakers, Methodists and other sects. In Fair Isle they have a population of 70, a Methodist minister, a chapel, and a Church of Scotland minister and church. The ministers take it in turns – one week the same congregation attend the Methodist chapel, the next week the Church of Scotland. This makes it easier for cleaners, flower-arrangers, crofters and others to cope with a very busy life and some very inclement weather. To sum up, in the words of Burleigh: 'The Church of Scotland has won and in large part retained the section of the Scottish people … moreover its tradition has been enriched by the devotion of the brave, good and sincere men and women who have left behind a heritage not to be lightly surrendered but rather to be conserved and increased and used in a new age of unexampled difficulty but also of splendid opportunity.'

Scottish Church Architecture

To compare the architecture of the Scottish church with that south of the border or in Wales is not possible. The buildings owe more to the influence of France, Norway and Denmark than to the Saxon, Norman and medieval influences from England. Even Symington, Ayrshire, with its three-light round-headed east window, dated 1160, is not easily recognisable now as it has a gallery and no separate chancel.

Scots Gothic usually had a cross design with the long arm being the nave, the shorter arm being the presbytery in abbey churches and in others the choir. The chancel was above the crossing and above the latter were the bells, usually in a tower with a crown, saddleback roof or occasionally a steeple. Sometimes the tower was at the west end. The window design can be listed as early single lancets, as at Symington where there is a group of three. Geometric designs had larger windows, with heads with simple geometric patterns. Curvilinear or flamboyant tracery comes next and then Perpendicular with mullions and transoms. Finally, there is intersecting-arc tracery (a pattern like intersecting diamonds in sixteenth- and seventeenth-century stone buildings, but in timber much later).

The Reformation did not stop Gothic buildings being built in Scotland but by the late sixteenth century churches were Protestant in style. The church at Dairsie is an exception, as Archbishop Spottiswood was following an English style, though with a very Scottish bell tower. The Presbyterians did not like it and it was stripped down in the 1640s and all unnecessary decoration removed.

In 1689, King William and Queen Mary left their chaplain, William Carstares, who was strongly influenced by the Dutch Protestant Church, to help Scotland to put Presbyterianism forward as the national religion. The Cameronians or Covenanters, who had opposed Dundee, disagreed and formed their own church, now called the Reformed Presbyterian Church, and the Episcopalians who did not really get their own buildings until the middle of the eighteenth century, remained as the Scottish Episcopalian Church.

Because the Presbyterians emphasised the preaching of the word, the pulpit became the focal point and the altar of communion table[1] was simply below the pulpit and unimportant in the service. Galleries were introduced as at Tenandry and Dowally (since removed) in Perthshire. St Peter's church at Sandwick[2] in Orkney, recently restored, has such a large pulpit that when one stands in the top position one's eye is at the level of the top gallery (no-one in the congregation would dare go to sleep). Judging by the long-bearded parson whose picture hangs on the wall, his voice would no doubt be loud enough to keep everyone's attention.

T-plan churches appeared (as at Maxton, Borders) and so as to get more people into the building extra galleries were built. The 'horseshoe' gallery appeared and at Kilarrow church, Bowmore on Islay, the church is round with a round gallery so that there is room for the whole village but, because of a central pillar supporting the conical roof, not everyone could see the pulpit.

By 1793 there was enough religious toleration to permit the Roman Catholic Church to emerge, especially in the Highlands and Western Isles, but there was little difference in the architectural styles. Town churches had porticos, spires (so they could be seen by their congregations) and sometimes walls of older churches were heightened to put in galleries. Roofs varied and some hipped or piended roofs appeared as at St Pauls, Perth. Some Gothic Revival chapels were built, like an Oxford or Cambridge chapel with seating on opposite sides. There was a need too for communion tables, usually lined with bench seats near the pulpit, or on occasions pews had folded fronts that opened out to form a table.

The growth of town populations meant that all sorts of churches appeared. The United Secession Church designed Classical-style buildings, some with pilaster fronts not porticos, and by the 1830s in Gothic Revival style. In the Highlands appeared the Parliamentary church, designed under the supervision of road- and bridge-maker Thomas Telford but designed in detail by William Thomson with four central doors and windows, 'Y' tracery, and lattice-style windows with cast-iron (not wood) tracery, all to a standard pattern. Iona's church and manse are excellent examples of this Parliamentary style and the original plans are visible for all in the church lobby.

By late Victorian times there were architects like John Kinross (the author's grandfather and namesake) who specialised in restoration work. Gordonstoun's Michael Kirk, created from a mausoleum, the Chapeltown Catholic Church in Morayshire, and restoration work at Falkland Palace Chapel, Straiton Parish Church in Ayrshire, and St Baldred's in North Berwick are his legacies.

Slightly later came the work of Peter MacGregor Chalmers. His work includes the Hoselaw Chapel, Borders, and the delightful, if underused, Protestant church on the Isle of Canna which has an Irish-style pencil tower. Originally Episcopalian, it is now Church of Scotland.

From the coming of the railways in the Victorian era, there was a new and unexpected addition to church building in Scotland. The 'tin' church was available by catalogue and could be shipped by rail (or ship) to the nearest rail-head or port. The congregation of Dalswinton in Dumfries and Galloway were quick off the mark and their tin church duly arrived and was bolted together at the edge of the wood just outside the village. There it still stands, painted red (rust-proof paint perhaps?) in all its glory. Other small tin churches included here are in the Highlands – Tomatin and Syre, both well looked after and serving useful functions. Today some are private houses or shops but they serve a purpose and, like the pre-fabs of the 1940s and 1950s, people have got to like and to cherish them, so that what seems temporary has become permanent.

Little was built during the Second World War. An exception is the amazing Italian Chapel in the Orkneys, a major tourist attraction today and yet surprisingly not on the cruise liners' coach tours.

Since then we have had some experimental buildings, starting with St Paul's Church, Glenrothes, designed by Metzstein and McMillan of Gillespie, Kidd and Coia. It has been called 'the most significant piece of architecture north of the English channel' but this was in *The Scotsman* of 1957 and this was when Coventry Cathedral was appearing in England. We may have loved it in 1957 but today our tastes have changed and there are buildings with less slab-like appearances and cold interiors around. As John Hume points out, many of the new churches with flat roofs had problems of maintenance, leaking roofs for a start. (Here in Hereford our modern church, St Francis, which had a flat roof has closed partly because of excessive maintenance costs.) However, I have included Rogerson and Spence's St Mary Tron church in Springburn which has been likened to a cheese in appearance but holds its own in spite of being surrounded by tower blocks.

What of the future? The outstanding church as far as I am concerned, in my extended trip round Scotland, is the Methodist, always-open church at Haroldswick, Unst, Shetland. Scandinavian in style and wooden-built, it is light, friendly, very practical and has (like seven of our churches in Herefordshire) a separate bell tower and comfortable chairs. We must look to re-shaping our congregational seating patterns to suit the service rather than the other way round. Space has to be adaptable, kitchens and toilets included tastefully, heating provided for cold days, air for hot days – those of us without much hair shouldn't have to put up with wall heaters that give us headaches – and the priest or preacher must be clearly heard. I think Haroldswick has solved all these problems very well as I cannot recall any steps, and any choir conductor there would be in seventh heaven. It is just a pity it is so far away.

Notes
1 Tokens were often sold for those taking communion.
2 Alas, too large for this book but it appears in Appendix 1.

ABERDEENSHIRE

There seem to be plenty of large churches in this county, but few small ones. Thanks to help from David Walker and others, I have chosen two:

1. St Lesmo's Chapel, Braeloine (Scottish Episcopal)

This is a very small private chapel on the Glen Tanar Estate near Aboyne. The estate was the seat of the late Lord Glentanar of the Coats thread family from Paisley.

The chapel is kept locked up (key in the estate office) but is used for weddings and christenings by the Episcopal Church. It was built by George Truefitt in 1872 and made of granite and slate, with inside pews lined with deerskin and unhewed timbers in the roof.

In the churchyard is a memorial to Sir William Cunliffe Brooks who imposed his Arts and Crafts ideas on many buildings in the area including this chapel. His gravestone is based on the design of the Kinord Pictish Cross.

St Lesmo, according to Butler's *Lives of the Saints*, was a Frenchman (d. AD 1100), soldier and monk who became Abbot of Burgos Abbey (now called Church of St Lesmos). He is also known as St Adelelmus. His feast day is 30 January.

2. Our Lady of the Snows, Tornahaish, Corgarff (Roman Catholic)

Situated on the A939 near its junction with the A944, this is a small chapel attached at right angles to a 1950s priest's house with a nice garden. The house is more for an overnight stay as the priest comes from the Roman Catholic church at Glengairden.

The interior is simple: board walls, original stone altar, wooden tabernacle and mid-nineteenth-century altar rails. Pews have panelled backs and some are original, others refitted. The north-east window was replaced in 2003, otherwise the windows are all original (1808).

St Lesmo's Chapel, Glentanar, Aberdeenshire. *Courtesy of Alison Poole*

Alisdair Roberts in *The Deeside Field* has written about the origins of this little chapel. It was the brainchild of Rev Lachlan McIntosh, who was minister here from 1783 until he died in 1847. He sat down and wrote letters asking for money to build the chapel, he himself contributing five precious guineas and his housekeeper £5. Only the £20 from Dr Chisholm, Bishop of the Highland District, can be considered a large sum and by 1808 the chapel was finished. By 1810 McIntosh was living in Ardoch, but still owing money for the chapel. It was hard going as there were never enough of the faithful to pay the bills. In 1844 the Rev William Mann was sent to help out and he records the shock of meeting Lachlan McIntosh.

I was humbled by the appearance of his low lodging and much edified by his great resignation to the poorness of his lot. On the Second Sunday after Easter he had been officiating at the chapel five miles above him, a journey which can now hardly be expected of him. He not only bends under the weight of 91 years, but is also subject to complaints (presumably medical) which give him a great deal of trouble. He is very emaciated and is represented to go through his Sunday duties with great difficulty.

When Lachlan died in 1847 at the age of 93 a good crowd turned up of which many he had baptised, and he was buried at St Mungo's churchyard at Foot of Gairn. The dedication of this place as 'Our Lady of the Snows' seems very appropriate and there must have been times when even the resolute, faithful Lachlan could not get through on his old pony.

When visited it seemed in need of some care. It is not normally open but one could try phoning St Margarets, Huntly (01466 792409) in advance. Corgarff near here has an unusual eighteenth-century castle to see.

The priest's house, built later, was for visiting clergy, supplied from Glengairden. The church interior has four original pews each side (seating 16) but others can be squeezed in if necessary on two additional pews and chairs. The east window (2003) has been dedicated to the Ross family with a blue Maltese cross and a three-leaf clover. There is also a very modern cross on the adjacent wall.

3. Towie Kirk, Glenkindie (Church of Scotland)

Just off the A97 south of Kildrummy Castle, Towie, is an 1803 church with four round-headed windows, a U-plan gallery on timber columns and a central pulpit with sounding board.

Towie Kirk, Aberdeenshire. *Courtesy of T. Coomber*

The glazing, four round-headed windows, date from 1803. The gable door is almost covered by two huge fir trees, trimmed like elders waiting to enter last. Like at Moy Kirk in Inverness-shire, there is no room in the churchyard for any more tombs. Towie is the parish church for Glenkindie. The west door has a fanlight as well as a round-topped window above this. There is a birdcage bellcote and in the centre of the roof ridge a small, stunted spiret which looks as if it had once been a chimney that has been capped by a toadstool enthusiast.

ARGYLL & BUTE

This is a straggly area of rugged coastline and numerous islands.

4. Ardentinny Parish Church (Church of Scotland)

Once a holiday village, Ardentinny is on Loch Long, and can be reached by taking the ferry to Dunoon. The church on the shore is a simple rectangular building of 1838 with a gabled front and porch, and bellcote at the gable apex. Inside it is plain with an ornamental sounding board over the preacher's pulpit and timber wall panels.

There are war memorials to the men of HMS *Armadillo*, the Royal Naval Commando unit which trained here. The village also has connections with Harry Lauder, Scottish singer and comedian, who used to sing he 'was coming o'er the hills to Ardentinny'. It is open daily and the Sunday service is at 2.00pm.

Ardentinny Church, Argyll & Bute. *Courtesy of A.R.N. Kinross*

AYRSHIRE

Forever associated with Robert Burns, this county also has Auchincruive College of Agriculture, which is not far from Symington, and we based ourselves there when looking at churches.

5. Symington Church, South Ayrshire (Church of Scotland)

This is not to be confused with another Church of Scotland church at Symington, Lanarkshire.

Basically Norman, it was founded by Symon de Loccard in 1160 and restored in 1919 by P. MacGregor Chalmers. The walls are three feet thick and the triple windows have some fine Strachan glass. There is a piscina, an open-work timber roof (rare in Scotland) and a gallery has been added for those who want to creep in late and leave early without anyone other than God knowing they are there.

Mr Nimmo has pointed out in the 1797 sketch of the seating plan that the pulpit has a desk in front of it where penitents sat during the service doing penance for sins committed. There may have been more than one in which case others sat nearby on small 'cutty' stools (with three legs). The larger the space the more it cost (one man paid up to £500 a year – a ploughman like Mr Burns only earned £18 a year then) and in the early twentieth century seat rents were still paid, half-yearly, so that in the back it cost 10s (50p) while in the front, where you had to stay awake, it was only 2s (10p). The letter 'D' on the plan indicates 'denizen of the parish.'

I spent some time trying to get into Symington Church, and was eventually let in by the Sessions Clerk. Thanks to the couple who let me in to phone this lady. For other visitors there are two phone numbers given in *Churches to Visit in Scotland* (No. 226).

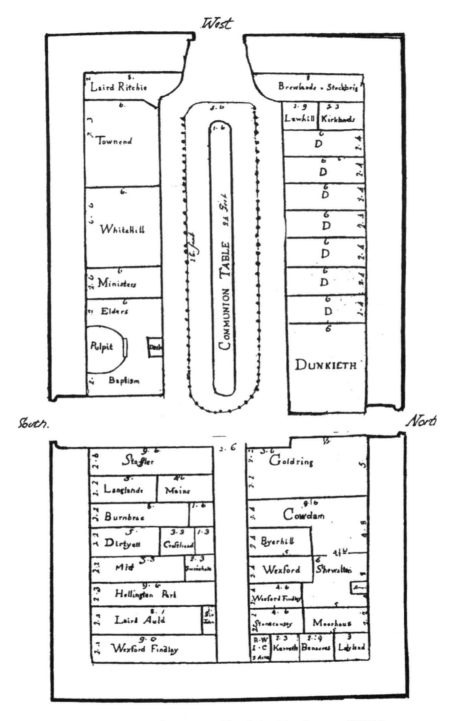

Seating arrangements of Symington Church, Ayrshire. *Courtesy of J.W. Nimmo*

BORDERS

Older readers will remember the original county names – Peeblesshire, Selkirkshire, Berwickshire and Roxburghshire.

Using Peebles as a base, I have included the following churches. Only Hoselaw Chapel is really small, but the others are of great interest and should not be missed. We walked from Peebles to Broughton on the John Buchan Way, saw Lyne on the way back and then the following day saw Hoselaw, Linton, Legerwood and Maxton.

6a. Hoselaw Chapel

Situated to the south-east of Kelso by Hoselaw Loch, this tiny chapel was built by P. MacGregor Chalmers in 1906 in memory of the minister and is rectangular, about 20ft by 13ft with a small apse. It appears disused although the *1000 Churches* says there is a 5th Sunday 12.15 service. The Willis window shows Our Lord holding the Sacramental Cup. This cup is copied from one in Weobley, Herefordshire's east window. The apse is painted with a fresco which shows angels in clouds on a blue background. It is in need of a bit of restoration. Linton Church is about a mile away.

6b. Linton Church

Linton is a little large for this book but Pevsner calls it 'one of the most significant Romanesque churches in the Borders' and is very much tied up with Hoselaw.

MacGregor Chalmers and Dr T. Leishman were responsible for its restoration. Like Lyne it is perched on top of a small hill, more of a chicken with chick than a single hen. It has a tympanum of St George slaying the dragon, which is hard to see. The light was in the wrong place when we called and we were busy supporting a lady who was determined her daughter (not present) should be married there and what did we think?

Linton Church, Borders

Interior, Linton Church, Borders

The nave has a monument to Major-General Walker (1840) and his brother who was a lieutenant-colonel. There is some fine 1936 glass by Douglas Strachan, a large south porch, a sundial on the south-west corner of the building and some good eighteenth-century memorials outside.

Presumably the lady would have to ask the owners of the rather grand former manse next door for permission to park all the wedding cars, and even then older guests would have a steep walk up to the church. If they come back for a christening, then there is a font that was once a blacksmith's 'small coal' store before it was found and brought back to the church. There is also a passing bell for funerals inscribed 'Linton, 1697, John Meikle *me fecit* Edinburgh'.

In 1977, Linton had its 850th anniversary and 20 trees were planted by 11 school children from the families Bryce, Elliot, Fleming, Hall and Welsh (two each), plus Marion Mann.

7. Legerwood Kirk

Legerwood is a small village in Berwickshire off the A68 between Lauder and Earlston. Note that Berwickshire is Scotland but Berwick-on-Tweed is part of Northumberland. The church is not in the village but tucked away in the middle of steadings, a school, manse and some converted barns. There was a priest here in 1127 but the building dates from before that time. At the Reformation the chancel was walled off and in 1804 an additional aisle added, making the building T-shaped. In 1989, W. van Vlack Lidgerwood restored the chancel and when we called, the interior had just been painted so all pews were covered in dust sheets giving an eerie look to the interior. The chancel arch of red sandstone, the nineteenth-century oculus with a small circular stained glass 'Light of the World' by Ballantine and Gardiner and underneath a single narrow 'Light of The Good Shepherd' are very effective. The altar has to be to the right of this as there is a large seventeenth-century monument to John Ker of Morriston and his wife Grizzell, 1748. It is Grizzell who is the real heroine of the village. She was the daughter of Sir John Cochrane, leader of the Ayrshire Covenanters. He was captured in 1685 and shut in Edinburgh's Tolbooth Jail. His daughter, dressed as a highwayman, intercepted the messenger bringing the death warrant from the king in the south, not once but twice, so that eventually Charles II reprieved Sir John. He had no idea that this mysterious highwayman was in fact his daughter, but the truth was eventually leaked out and the two reunited. What her husband and family thought about the business we

Legerwood Kirk, Borders

don't know and whether any of her family took part in the '45 Rising and survived is not known, but it is a fascinating story some of which is told on the monument in the chancel.

Outside there is a corner sundial as at Linton (1689) and amongst the tombs, a table tomb of Rev Calderwood (1709) who was minister in Grizzell's time. The church seems in very good shape. It is usually open and there is a monthly service at 11.45 on the first Sunday of the month.

8. Lyne Kirk (Church of Scotland)

Perched up on a hill like a fat contented chicken, Lyne Church is nowhere near Lyne Station (trains closed by Dr Beeching) but it is easy to find. Park near the main road and walk up as there is no turning area at the top of the lane.

This is a seventeenth-century building, unusual for Scotland, although a church here may have existed in the twelfth century. John Hay of Yester helped build the new church and inside his family pews are at the rear of the nave with little canopies and his initials on one of them. He became the first Earl of Tweeddale. There is a Dutch wooden pulpit and a pre-Reformation font.

Outside (the Peebles side) is a tomb that is carefully protected by a screen. On one side is an Adam and Eve carving and on the other the words: 'Life is the road to death & death Heaven's gate must be. Heaven is the thron(e) of Christ and Christ is love to me. Jane Veitch, daughter of John Veitch … died 13 of Jan 1712 aged 16'.

In the vestry I saw a model of the Roman fort nearby and a colour photo of the lady minister and her congregation on 5 November 1989, the day the roof was completed and the building re-opened. It was found that the seventeenth-century roof had no nails only oak dowels in the sarking. The 1888 repairs had used hand-made nails forged at Lyne Smithy.

The wall at the back of the bell turret has two graves to members of the Taggart family who are also remembered inside. Alas, they were local church folk not Glasgow policemen. Services are at 11.00am on the first Sunday of the month.

Lyne Kirk, Borders

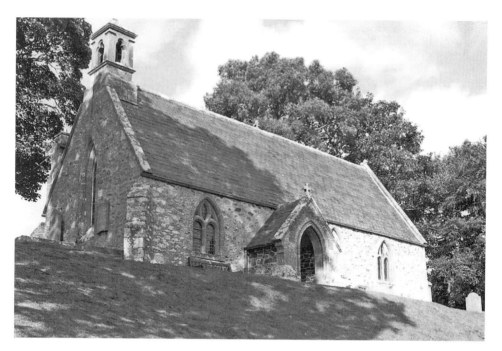

Lyne Kirk, Borders. Taggart monuments are on the bell turret wall. *Copyright J. Rogers*

One of the saviours of Lyne in Victorian times was the Earl of Wemyss who was a member of the Tweeddale Shooting Club. In 1822, the Club had decided that four acres of Lyne farm should be turned into a cover for hare coursing. In December 1822 it was decided in the Club minutes that this area should be 'planted with trees, sown with whins and broom and enclosed with a stone dyke five feet high'. The same minutes note that the money was paid out to the Procurator Fiscal and two men for apprehending and prosecuting poachers. It was the 11th Earl of Wemyss, who was MP for Haddington and later Ipswich, who gave money to repair the church, but it was his grandfather, the 9th Earl who was besotted with country sports and the Club Memoir says 'he scarcely knew which gave him the greater excitement, killing a difficult fox or securing a 40lb salmon in very turbid water'.

9. Maxton Parish Church

Maxton is close to St Boswells on the A699 about 20 minutes from Kelso. The church is down a lane by a field which was being ploughed when we arrived. The kind lady in the terracotta cottage provided the key.

Maxton Parish Church, Borders. *Courtesy of Alison Poole*

From outside there is perfect symmetry like a Parliamentary church, with two doors west and east, two central round windows and an oculus in the centre. The west gable has a birdcage bellcote. There is a north aisle added in 1866 and, as you enter, a useful kitchen and a toilet added in 1962.

Interior fittings date from 1812 when Alexander Kinghorne set about some restoration work. Everything is immaculate and the pale grey paint adds to the peaceful atmosphere. The north wall window is by J.H. Coram, 1914, and there is an oval tablet to the Kers of Littledean.

On one wall is a picture of HMS *Maxton*, a coastal minesweeper of the 'Ton' class launched in 1956. Judging by its size, I was glad I was travelling to the Hebrides by a slightly larger ferry.

Outside there is a corner sundial. There are services here at 11.30am on the 2nd and 4th Sundays. The church is on the St Cuthbert Way[1] and is dedicated to St Cuthbert. According to *1000 Churches* it was a thatched church until 1790.

Notes
1 The St Cuthbert Way is a walking route from Melrose to Lindisfarne

THE JOHN BUCHAN SOCIETY

Hon Secretary: Glennis McClemont
37 Waterloo Road, Lanark MLII7QH
2000@yahoo.co.uk

The John Buchan Society was formed about 15 years ago to promote the works of the famous Scottish author. Every year they hold a weekend AGM and conference, sometimes in Scotland and sometimes in England. Their 'headquarters' in Scotland is the disused free church at Calzeat to the south of Broughton on the A701 Edinburgh–Moffat road.

Here John Buchan came as a boy and for a time his father was minister. One of the windows is dedicated to the Hannay family. The church was 'Gothicised' in 1892 by R. Bryden and the stained glass is by Ballantine and Gardiner. Nowadays it is a museum dedicated to John Buchan's life and there are always some of his books on sale here.

It is a good example of how to make use of a redundant church building on a main road. The fireplace, Victorian, was removed from the Buchan house in Peebles and set up in the church.

We visited on a Sunday morning having walked over from Peebles on the John Buchan Way, a long distance path of about 13 miles, which on a fine day is the best way to get there. From Broughton it is a short trip to Lyne Church (see page 35).

The John Buchan Museum, Borders

DUMFRIES & GALLOWAY

These two counties cover a large area. Galloway is noted for its 'Belted Galloway' cattle but they seem scarce there today. Galloway used to consist of Wigtownshire and Kirkcudbrightshire.

10. Dalswinton (Tin) Church

Built in 1881 with Gothic windows and an east spire containing a bellcote, Dalswinton is rust red in colour and seems to be floodlit at night although standing at the edge of a wood outside the village. In 2008, it had no notice of any services or of any key holder. Inside there is a west window (1975) by Cyril Watson showing the Life of David and an earlier 1950 stained-glass window on the north wall.

There is a service (10.00am) twice a month on the second and fourth Sundays and you can phone 01387 710572 for a key.

EDINBURGH

11. St Bennet's Chapel, 42 Greenhill Gardens, Edinburgh (Roman Catholic)

The second smallest chapel in Edinburgh, after St Margaret's, is St Bennet's. Situated north of Bruntsfield Park it is easy to find. However, do not try to get in through the front door as it is not used. Try the door next to it and the housekeeper will show you round. St Bennet's is the private chapel of the Archbishop of St Andrews and Edinburgh. Currently this is Cardinal O'Brien.

Inside the chapel, Byzantine in style, are four arches under a dome. There is some fine 1970 glass by Gabriel Loire of Chartres. They depict

St Bennet's Chapel, Edinburgh

St Margaret, St Andrew and the Crucifixion. Pevsner calls them the 'finest post-war glass in Edinburgh'. The other windows in this chapel depicting St Ninian and St Columba are very modern and not easy to make out.

Schultz designed the chapel furnishing – normal practice in 1907 – and the gilt chair came from McIntosh of Kirkcaldy at the time of the Pope John Paul visit to the chapel in 1982. Note the coat of arms of the Archdiocese of St Andrews and Edinburgh on the banner. In the old days this would have been taken to a field of battle to inspire the troops.

The chapel is used regularly when the Archbishop is at home. It is also visited by children from 40 primary schools. When I lived in this part of Edinburgh in 1960 I had no idea it existed, so it is one of the treasures of Edinburgh worth discovering.

12. St Margaret's Chapel

The highest point of the Castle Rock, and approached through the main gate, is the little chapel dedicated to St Margaret. It measures about 28ft x 16ft on the outside. Inside it is plastered with a tunnel-vaulted nave and five wonderful, small windows by Douglas Strachan (c.1922) showing William Wallace, Ss Andrew, Ninian and Columba and, in the east, St Margaret herself.

Who was St Margaret? She was born in Hungary, the granddaughter of Edmund Ironside and daughter of Edward the Exile, c.1046. Her mother was Princess Agatha, probably daughter of King Stephen of Hungary. In 1054 Edward was summoned by the Witan to return to England and replace Edward the Confessor as king. However, Edward died on arrival and his unprotected family remained at the English court, as Harold was lined up to become king. Margaret, with her brother, Edgar Atheling, sailed for the Continent in 1066 but their ship was driven up to Fife by contrary winds, landing at St Margaret's Hope (not be be confused with the one in Orkney). She was welcomed by King Malcolm III, who had met Margaret when she was a child. In 1070 they were married and she encouraged the Christian Church in Scotland, guaranteeing free passage of the Forth for pilgrims going to St Andrews (hence North and South Queensferry). She is reputed to have built the chapel, though the present building is a bit later than 1093 when she died. Her body was taken to Dunfermline Abbey to be buried in state and she was canonised in 1250.

My chief memory of the chapel is attending a wedding there in the 1970s and being given the responsibility of escorting the bride's mother (in high heels) across the snowy cobbles to the castle room for the reception (in my leather-soled shoes) with a high and very cold wind. We made it but alas I had no time to look at the chapel.

Returning later I was impressed by the flowers. They are placed in the chapel by the Guild of Margarets who look after the chapel, though the guide said she sometimes has to rearrange them as not all Margarets are gifted with the art of flower-arranging. This chapel is not to be overlooked by those visiting the castle. For the disabled or poor walkers, you can get a taxi to the castle tournament yard and then get a strong person to escort you up the hill.

FIFE

There are one or two contenders for the smallest church in Fife. The Palace of Falkland's Chapel, restored in Edwardian times and still used by local Catholics, is one, and the little Episcopal church at Ladybank another. A friend tells me she attended a service at the latter, where the congregation was offered a cup of tea afterwards. The kettle was plugged into a nearby plug (used for the heating too) and the water was lifted in a handy container over the fence from next door. Such are the beauties of worship in Scotland today. However, from an architectural point of view, you should go and see:

13. Dairsie Old Parish Church (Church of Scotland)

On the A91 between Cupar and Guardbridge, Dairsie is a church built by Archbishop Spottiswoode in 1621. A relation of the Archbishop calls it 'Ane of the beautifulest little pieces of churchwork' and another comment says 'A piece of cold mimicry like the work of the cabinet maker rather than of the architect'.

Sited above the river, it is certainly above average for a village church. It has four hood-moulded three-light windows with buttresses and a unique corner tower, a spire and some gargoyle water spouts that pre-date the piended roof (1794). The building was restored by Kennedy and MacCullochin in 1835-37. The interior is much altered from the Archbishop's original design – the screen and Royal coat-of-arms no longer being present – but it is well worth a visit.

In the churchyard are a simple Gothic session house and some table tombs, one dated from 1722. The nearby castle ruins are where the young King David III lived in his minority and where in 1335 the Scottish Estates met. Later it was the home of the Learmont family.

Archbishop Spottiswoode, who planned Dairsie Church, said he 'publicly and upon his own charges built and adorned the church of Darsy after the English form as one of the beautifullest little pieces of church work that is left to that now unhappy country.' He was writing in 1621 when the episcopacy was not popular. He, as a supporter of Charles I, fled to England

Dairsie Church in the late nineteenth century. *Engraved by R.W. Billings*

when the Covenanters came to power. He died in 1639 and King Charles I, according to the Scottish historian Lang and mindful of Dairsie, said:

> Our father of blessed memory immediately after his coming into England compared the decency and uniformity of God's worship here with that diversity, nay deformity, which was used in Scotland, where no set of public form of prayers was used, but Preachers or Readers and ignorant Schoolmasters prayed in the church, sometimes so ignorantly that it was a shame to have the Majesty of God so barbarously spoken unto; sometimes so seditiously that their prayers were plain libels girding at sovereignty and authority; or lies being stuffed with all the reports in the Kingdom.

Dairsie is not used today but is periodically opened for visitors.

GLASGOW

14. St Mary, Tron Parish Church, 128 Red Road, Springburn (Church of Scotland)

Originally, the smallest church in Glasgow was probably St Barnabas in Dennistoun but it closed down in the 1980s and the congregation (Episcopal) moved elsewhere.

There are few others to suggest in Glasgow as small. One such is St Mary, Tron Parish Church in Springburn, designed by Rogerson and Spence in 1964-6. A 'tron' is a public weighing beam and the central Tron Kirk is now the Tron Theatre, so from an ecclesiastical point of view Springburn's Tron Church takes over. Pevsner describes it as 'a little grey harled building overwhelmed by neighbouring tower blocks'.

St Mary, Glasgow. *Courtesy of Alison Poole*

Christianity with a capital 'C' is prevalent at St Mary's Church. Many of the congregation are asylum seekers who speak no English (or Scots) and the Rev Jill Clancy runs the English conversation classes with child care and organises special services for them. There is also a drop-in centre. The building may be ugly – my son has described it as a pebble-dash flat-roofed nuclear bunker next to a Chinese take-away complete with tall thin windows and a metal cross – but at heart it is filling a need in this area where there are plenty of lost souls.

The architects, Rogerson & Spence, are mainly responsible for designing public libraries as at Hillhead and Govanhill. They were also responsible for Victoria Park Parish Church near the Clyde Tunnel (1968/70) which had to be built on changing levels and is unfortunately of blue engineering brick and concrete. It does boast a small chapel off the foyer.

Another building which is a long way from churches or public libraries, but someone had to design it, so why not Rogerson & Spence, is the Shieldhall sewage works of 1980. Springburn is well known as being a centre for the building of railway locomotives but, although on the main Edinburgh to Glasgow line, it has lost its industry and now sprouts tower blocks.

INVERNESS-SHIRE

15. Moy Kirk, Inverness-shire (Church of Scotland)

Off the A9, just short of Inverness, Moy Kirk is on the edge of the old road and dates from 1765. Pevsner considers that the round arched windows and birdcage bellcote date from 1829 when the building was repaired. I have never seen so many tombstones crammed into a small walled churchyard as at Moy Kirk. Jutting out from the west wall is one to Aeneas Mackintosh (their laird lives just up the road in Moy Hall) who was an army officer in Keith's Regiment who served in Germany, but put on half-pay in 1763 at the Peace Treaty at the end of the Seven Years War.

Moy is famous for the Rout of Moy. In February 1746, Bonnie Prince Charlie was staying at Moy Hall as a guest of Lady Mackintosh. The Earl of Loudoun, commander of the Hanoverian forces in Inverness, took 1500

Moy Kirk, Inverness-shire

Tomatin (Tin) Church, Inverness-shire

men to attempt to capture the prince. One of the Mackintosh clan gave the warning and Lady Mackintosh sent out her local blacksmith, Donald Fraser, and five men armed with muskets. They hid in a thicket overlooking Loudoun's route. When the latter approached, his piper Macrimmon was shot and the small group of defenders put up such a noise with shouting for imaginary clans to intercept the invaders that the latter beat a hasty retreat, not just to Inverness but over the Kessock ferry into the Black Isle. After Culloden, 'Colonel Anne', as Lady Mackintosh was named, was briefly arrested. The tomb of Donald Fraser is in the graveyard.

For the key of this church, contact Rev Campbell at Daviot Manse in the next village or try Mrs V. Roden (01808 511355).

16. Tomatin (Tin) Church, Inverness-shire

Erected in 1910 and painted blue-green, this tin church is up a bank on the old A9. It was originally a United Free Church but is now Church of Scotland. Services are held from April to October, on second and fourth Sundays at 10.30am.

The key holder is Mrs V. Roden (01808 511355).

LOCHABER

Lochaber, now just a district, is famous, amongst other things, for being on the road to the Isles.

17. St John, Ballachulish (Scottish Episcopal)

Situated on the shore of Loch Leven near to Glencoe, this church is 'stark and granite' according to Pevsner, its cruciform style dating from 1842, with the chancel added by David Mackintosh in 1888. It has a huge churchyard and one of the graves is to Major A.S. MacDonald MM who was one of three Argylls who escaped from the Germans in 1940 and when recaptured spoke Gaelic to his two friends. They pretended to be Russian workers and 'after many vicissitudes' reached Spain where they were 'smuggled home'.

Even during the Forty-Five Rising a majority of the Jacobite army were members of the Episcopalian Church, and in the early days Stewart of Ballachulish gave up his storehouse to be used as a chapel, and so it was not until 1842 that Peter McNab, an Oban architect, designed the new church. In 1871 the local bishop wrote to a friend, 'we had the most crowded church on Sunday I ever saw at Ballachulish – many could not get in'. Today, 30 is considered a good number.

The rather unusual altar and reredos were the work of J.W.M. Wedderburn and date from the same time as the chancel whose three end windows have an unusual design rather like a railway arch repeated, the keystone being orange or green. Under the chancel floor is buried Mary McKenzie, wife of Kenneth McKenzie, a merchant: 'Aged 55 years. Deeply regretted'. Altogether this is a church worth a stop.

ROSS-SHIRE

Part of Ross and Cromarty and now Highland.

18. St Maelrubha, Poolewe (Scottish Episcopal)

The village of Poolewe is visited by tourists who go to see the famous Inverewe Gardens (National Trust for Scotland), but if you arrive after 4.00pm the tea shop has closed, so find the Episcopal church, a former cow byre, where you will be made welcome.

William Glashan converted it in 1965 and now it makes a long thin building, 42ft x 13ft, with seating for 54. There are unplastered walls and an open king-post roof.

The nearby Church of Scotland building has recently been sold off as a private dwelling. It appears in Pevsner (1992) *Highlands and Islands*.

Who is St Maelrubha you may ask? He was a Pictish apostle from Ireland who became a monk in Bangor, Co. Down, in *c*.AD 671. He founded a monastery in Applecross (Ross and Cromarty) and built a church on Loch Maree's island which became famous for healing people. His feast day is 21 April. He lived until the age of 80.

Not in the guide book at Inverewe is this little story:

The Church of Scotland minister was walking in Inverewe Gardens when he met the gardener, a Mr MacGregor. 'This garden is a credit to you', said the priest, 'but of course it would be nothing without the work of the Lord'. MacGregor thought a while, then replied, 'Aye, Minister, but did you see it when the good Lord had it all to himself?'

Interior of St Maelrubha Church. *Courtesy of Alison Poole*

SUTHERLAND

This northern county of Scotland is, strangely, called 'Sutherland'.

19. Croick Parish Church, Sutherland (Church of Scotland)

Not easy to find, Croick is at the far end of Strathcarron, which is reached by turning off the A9 onto the A386 near Tain and following the road west as far as it goes.

The church stands alone with a few trees around it and dates from 1825. It is used about once a year and has a long communion table, stone flags, a high pulpit and sounding board, a small stove and Tudor-style windows.

Originally there were 450 parishioners but Glen Calvie was part of the Highland Clearances and the Duke of Sutherland preferred sheep to people, so 80 locals were packed up and sent to Ardgay, Edderton and Shandwick in Ross and Cromarty. This was 1843 and some of them, unable to get in the church, carved rescue messages on the windows which are still visible.

In 1727, Janet Macleod was born here. She was famous as the 'fasting woman', living until the age of 70 but only eating enough food for a two-year-old. The church is a Parliamentary design (by William Thomson rather than Thomas Telford) and so too the manse nearby which is now a keeper's lodge.

20. Eriboll Church, Sutherland (Church of Scotland)

This little church stands isolated on the A838, to the east side of Loch Eriboll, on the very north coast of Scotland. It has two lights, a large porch and a very small vestry. Built in 1804, it originally had a spirelet on the east gable. There used to be lime kilns in this part and maybe the church was built for kiln workers. In 2009 when at the Pitlochry theatre, I noticed a picture of this church by the artist Sue Challis. It now hangs on my study wall as I write this piece.

Sue Challis (who painted the picture that appears on the front cover of this book) has commented on Eriboll Church. Originally a mission church, it was closed in the 1970s as the congregation had vanished and the local estate looked after it. However, a viable community was built up in the area so that the church is now used on occasions, chiefly for weddings. Inside it is very plain, just one 'artisan' stained-glass window, austere and solidly built and seems in good repair. Sheep keep the grass around it nice and trim and the Presbytery Clerk at Hope keeps an eye on it. It is a very special place.

21. Strathnaver (Tin) Church, Syre

Another Spiers of Glasgow building, built in 1901 with a rust-red roof, white walls and a tall street lamp outside. It was a mission church with a priest from Altnahara to serve the estate workers in Sutherland. It was originally a United Free Church but in 1929 it joined up with the Church of Scotland. It has a plaque in memory of Rev R. Sloan, minister here from 1969-74. Near here is Rossal clearance village. Services are at 3.00pm on the second, fourth and fifth Sundays of the month. It is open at all times and can be found at the junction of the Syre and Kinbrace roads.

THE WEE FREES

Visitors to the Outer Hebrides are often puzzled by exactly who the Wee Frees are. The first schism in the Church of Scotland of any note occurred in 1843. The Free Church was formed, rejecting patronage and encouraging a more evangelistic approach to worship. This appealed to Highlanders and Islanders alike. In 1893, to confuse things, the Free Presbyterian Church of Scotland was formed by two ministers in the Highlands. They did not agree with the Free Church ideas, especially their Declaratory Act, 1892, when it was seen that the Free Church, by supporting it, were being disloyal to the original confession of faith they made in 1843. Many Free Church ministers left in 1900 to form the United Free Church of Scotland. The rump of the Free Church then repealed the Declaratory Act and it is this body which is known as the Wee Frees.

The film *Whisky Galore*, made on Barra in the 1940s, has a famous scene in which the fishermen set out to rescue the whisky but one of them stops and says 'T'is the Sabbath' and they all return home. When we went to Stornaway we were careful not to take the newly introduced Sunday ferry so as not to upset the Islanders who still consider Sunday a complete day of rest, whether or not they consider themselves Wee Frees.

CANNA

Canna is managed by the National Trust for Scotland. It is next to the islands of Rhum and Eigg and is reached by ferry from Mallaig.

One of the most pleasant of the small inhabited islands of the Inner Hebrides, Canna covers 3247 acres and has a population of 24, including a farm, post office, tiny school, and no less than three churches. It is reached from Mallaig. The harbour has a huge jetty, big enough to get a couple of coaches ashore side by side. Alas, it has no road for cars, just a track suitable for Land Rovers or tractors – and walkers.

22. Scots Kirk

This is the first building reached from the harbour. It has an Irish-style pencil-thin tower and inside is a pointed tunnel-shaped roof with chapel-like seating for about 30, and a lectern. When not used by the Church of Scotland (the inhabitants are mostly Catholics) there is a display for tourists. It was built in 1911 as a memorial church for the Thoms, owners then of Canna, by P. MacGregor Chalmers.

23. St Columba's Chapel

The original chapel, now a ruin, is further up the hill near the site of the one-armed cross and punishment stone. On the next door island of Sanday (walking distance) stands the disused small church of St Edward the Confessor which has an unsafe roof and is firmly locked. In 1963, the Island Catholics decided to move the post office into a wooden shed (like a pre-war cricket pavilion) and move the Roman Catholic services into the post office. This building (c.1770) had been a chapel before 1887 and now it is again, very smartly set out with a lot of pale blue and comfortable seats for about 36 islanders.

Nearby is a lonely phone box (still working with coins) and a pillar box where I posted a card home. Two weeks after I returned (to England) the card turned up, having been found in the phone box and re-routed. Thank you to the islander who carried out this service for me. I expect it was the same lady who served us all ice cream from her kitchen freezer. Islanders are kind people, none more so than those on Canna.

The track continues over a bridge, originally built in 1905, but destroyed in a gale in the winter of 2005. The new bridge, wide enough for small vehicles, was built in 2006 and beside the Sanday end is a shrine to Mary constructed by a monk from Pluscarden Abbey in 1950.

St Columba's Chapel, Canna

FAIR ISLE

24/25. Church of Scotland and Methodist Chapel

Situated between Shetland and Orkney, Fair Isle does not mean that the weather is fair. The name is a derivation from Old Norse *feoer-oy* or far off. To stay there you must reserve a place at the Bird Observatory, currently being rebuilt (set up by George Waterston in the 1960s when the island became owned by the National Trust for Scotland). Then you have to book a place on the *Good Shepherd* which sails three times a week from Sumburgh on Shetland. The alternative for those not keen on rough seas in small boats is a small plane that flies from Tingwall Airport on Shetland (Logan Air). You get allotted a seat according to your weight and I was next to the pilot which was like being back in the RAF. My wife was in the air-gunner's position and we had a couple of painters and decorators on board who insisted on us dive-bombing the house they were to work on so they could assess the size of the roof.

The island is only 1898 acres and has about 70 inhabitants so that the church is easy to find. Beware, though, as the same congregation attend chapel and church alternatively. The minister (whose wife used to run the school at one time) doubles with the lay preacher who takes the Methodist Chapel services. Hymns are sung with great gusto and there is much talk afterwards. One member of the congregation (a young man) was in a wheelchair when we were there (2007) and his minder was so busy talking that she did not notice the wheelchair moving down the path where it would have picked up speed and gone quickly and disastrously over the cliff. It went over my foot, but luckily someone younger and fitter sped after it and stopped it as it went through the open gate.

The chapel windows were commissioned by Thomas Wilson, an islander who made his money in Australia during the Gold Rush. They are by Ballantine & Son of Edinburgh and it was the son James who designed them in 1936. The kirk windows, fine scenes of island life, are more modern. They were designed and made by Patrick Ross-Smith who was originally commissioned just to clean the chapel windows but decided to settle on the island. Jerry Stout from Leough commissioned them in memory of his wife

Aggie. Patrick also worked at Scalloway Castle, Shetland, and on the Chapter House in Elgin Cathedral. His glass deserves more praise and everyone who visits Fair Isle should make a point of seeing it for it is inspirational.

When Sinclair and Hardie designed the church in 1892 all the building blocks were dumped in the South Harbour as there was no quay on which to land them. The chapel, built a few years earlier, has two 1936 stained-glass windows, which alas I didn't see as services were being held in the church on the Sunday I was there.

In the Armada (1588), the Spanish ship *El Gran Grifon*, 38 guns, was wrecked at Sivars Geo, but most of the crew (200 men) were rescued by the islanders and fed until they could be sent to Shetland. Spain never forgot this act of hospitality and in 1984 a delegation dressed as Conquistadors arrived and planted an iron cross in the churchyard to commemorate those who died. It was a cuckoo operation as the islanders – less than 200 – had very little food to live on themselves. Fair Isle is an experience not to be missed whether or not you are an ornithologist.

Fair Isle Kirk, with the ferry crossing in the background. *Photograph by and copyright of Dave Wheeler*

HEBRIDES

The islands can be reached by ferry from Oban, Uig or Ullapool, or by air to Benbecula. We went from Ullapool to Lewis but returned from Barra to Oban.

LEWIS

Most of the islanders here are Protestant and churches of other denominations are hard to find. However, for small church enthusiasts the obvious first building to find is:

26. St Moluag's, Eoropie, Ness (Scottish Episcopal)

'Yorr-opp-ee', as it is pronounced, is right at the end of the A857 near the Butt of Lewis. The place is also spelled 'Eoropaidh' as you are now in a Gaelic-speaking area. The little church is at the end of a long footpath.

Measuring only 44ft x 18ft it is T-shaped with a massive tiled roof so that one approaches it from the side and it looks as if you are walking into a barn. It used to be a place of pilgrimage for the healing of sores and insanity. To the south is a little lean-to chapel with a squint into the main altar, so that it could be used by the sick. On the north side is a locked sacristy. The plan is like that of Gardar Church, Greenland. Pevsner reckons it dates from the thirteenth century. Restored in 1912, it is used by the priest of St Peter's, Stornaway, or by a local Reader, Donald McKee, who was kind enough to point out that if you leave your car at the end of the footpath and walk towards the radio aerial you will find the village tea-shop (run by a Nottingham lady) which, when one is recovering from a rough crossing, is welcome indeed.

St Moluag is another spelling of Maelrubha (see page 51) and inside the font the cross comes from the Flannan Islands, but the Prayer Tree is new and on it we found a letter from a child saying 'Please pray for Uncle Roddy's soar knee'.

St Moluag's, Eoropie, Lewis. *Drawing supplied by D. McKee*

The saintly Ronan, a monk who lived near Eoropie, who is mentioned by Bede, found the noise of the scolding women in the village too much to cope with, so he prayed God would send him to a distant land where he could no longer hear their voices. The next day a voice told him to go to Ness beach where he found a large whale which carried him to the island of North Rona, where he built his chapel, still visible as a ruin today although St Ronan lived in the eighth century. There was no noise of scolding women when we were there and those we met were most helpful in directing us to the little church.

27. Christ Church, Harris (Scottish Episcopal & Roman Catholic)

A few miles south of Tarbert, this little church was constructed out of a double garage by a local architect. It is used by both the local members of the Episcopal Church and at a different time by the Roman Catholics, who have a church in Stornaway. Really small, Christ Church has a meeting room with an altar that can be screened off. The cross is picked out in the window on tinted glass which reminds me of the Fitzwilliam Chapel in Cambridge where Sir Richard MacCormac achieved the same effect.

There is also a small chapel on the island of Ensay (off Leverburgh) which is run by Christ Church Episcopalians. There is no point in visiting it without the key as it is only used on rare occasions and then by the Christ Church congregation who keep the key.

For entry to Christ Church it is best to attend a service on a Sunday. The Episcopalians meet in the morning and the Catholic Mass is at 5.00pm.

NORTH UIST

The Uists are rather like the skeleton of a fish, with Benbecula in the middle connected by causeways. Eriskay is a tiny blob hanging on at the bottom. Then there is the round bigger blob of Barra and attached to it an apple core which is Vatersay. There are still four islands below this, the largest of which, Mingulay, I visited. It has the remains of a Victorian school – still with three outside WCs – that has been turned into a shelter. There are ruined cottages, a ruined church and a wonderful beach where two seals were lying looking at us humans wondering why we had come.

28. Lochmaddy Kirk (Church of Scotland)

Open and welcoming, this kirk seems well used. There were pots of heather on the windowsills and in the small chapel next door some much more comfortable chairs. Pevsner dates it to 1891 and says it was originally a Free Church.

Interior, Lochmaddy Kirk, North Uist

St Joseph's, Howbeg, South Uist

SOUTH UIST

29. St Brides, West Gerinish (Roman Catholic)

A small church approached from the A865 in the north of South Uist. It has
a Mass at 7.30pm on a Saturday. There is the statue by Hew Lorimer of Our
Lady of the Isles near here which one can see. It is rather overshadowed by
the later Ministry of Defence aerials on the hill behind.

30. St Joseph, Howbeg

Not to be confused with Howmore and it is Tobha Beag on my Ordnance
Survey map – fine for Gaelic speakers – so to find it you have to trek down
some windy lanes. It is smaller than St Brides, has some nice wooden
panelling with a Saturday Mass at 6.00pm. Nearby is a much larger white
painted Church of Scotland kirk and a collection of old ruined buildings,
some thatched, which are slowly being restored.

Milton village is also close by and you can see a monument in a ruined farmhouse to Flora MacDonald who was born here. She set out from South Uist on her famous voyage to Skye with a gawky Betty Burke maidservant, who was Prince Charlie in disguise.

31. St Michael's, Eriskay (Roman Catholic)

Reached from South Uist by a causeway, the church is on top of the hill as you get to the island on the right of the road.

It is a Gothic 1903 building with striking white-painted window margins and an apse. The south-west porch has a bellcote. Inside, there is a west gallery and room for all the islanders. The altar has the prow of a lifeboat in it (from a Royal Navy ship) and there are real anchors to left and right. Outside is the bell from the German First World War ship *Derfflinger*, which was scuttled in Scapa Flow, but rescued and then scrapped. The bell came from a yard in Glasgow that sold it to the clergyman who presented it to St Michael's Church. However, the real bell is in a museum in Germany, so there is a mystery about this one. Perhaps German battle-cruisers had two bells?

Interior of St Michael's, Eriskay (1903) showing the boat prow altar

1 St Margaret's Chapel, Edinburgh Castle

2 The Michael Kirk, Gordonstoun

3 Dalswinton Mission Church, Dumfries & Galloway

4 St Kilda Kirk and School

5 The Scots Kirk, Canna

6 Italian Chapel, Lamb Holm, Orkney

7 Our Lady of the Snows, Corgarff

8 Lunna Church, Shetland

9 Church of Scotland, Fair Isle

10 Interior of Kirk, Fair Isle

11 St Michael's, Eriskay

12 Telford Parish Church, Iona

13 St Oran's Chapel, Iona

14 St Columba's Shrine with the shadow of St John's Cross. *Courtesy and copyright of Historic Scotland*

15 St Moluag's, Eoropie, Lewis

16 Inside St Moluag's, Lewis

17 MacNeil coat of arms, Kisimul Castle, Barra. *J. Stainton*

18 Fortinghall Church, Perthshire

19 The approach to St Boniface, Papa Westray, Orkney

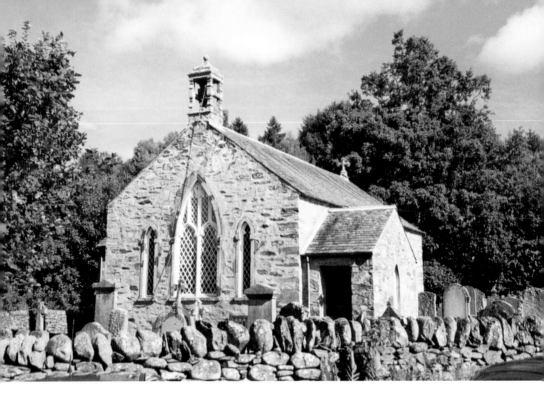

Above: 20 St Anne, Dowally, Perthshire

Left: 21 St Maelrubha's, Poolewe

Right: 22 Christ Church, Harris – the altar with sliding doors

Below: 23 Maxton, Borders, the interior

24 Pulpit at St Boniface, Papa Westray, with accordion case underneath

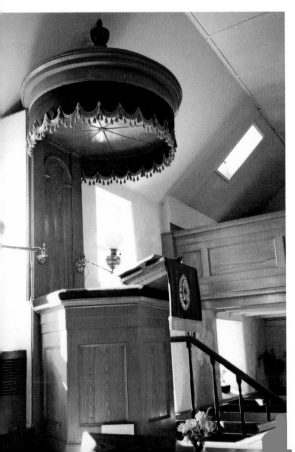

25 Pulpit at Lunna. Note curtain pelmet above

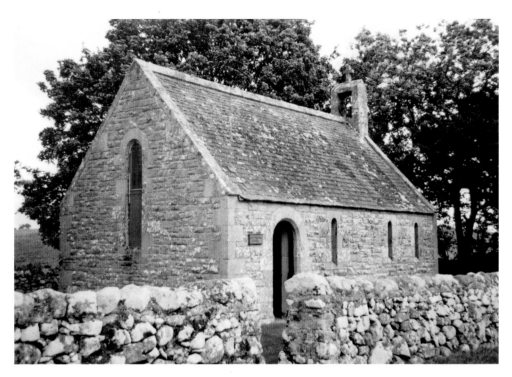

26 Hoselaw Chapel, Borders

27 The apse, Hoselaw

28 Towie Kirk, Aberdeenshire. *T. Coomber*

ISLE OF BARRA, OUTER HEBRIDES

This little island, mostly inhabited by Roman Catholics, can be reached by ferry from Oban, by air from Glasgow (the plane lands on the beach) or by ferry from Eriskay.

The island of Whisky Galore is only 45 minutes away by the small ferry. The island of Vatersay is joined by a causeway so that in July 2009 the fishing fleet was blessed by Canon McQueen and Father Michael with Mr MacNeil from Portree, Father Tony from Glasgow and Father George from Dumbarton attending. It was the combined fleet of Barra and Vatersay that was blessed flying their Scottish saltires. It was all filmed by a German film crew for some strange reason.

32. St Vincent de Paul, Eoligarry (Roman Catholic)

Beyond the airport, this is a 1964 building with a very tall roof. Nearby is a cemetery at Cille Bharra (named after St Finbarr) where there is Compton MacKenzie's tombstone as well as a small ruined chapel with a new roof over a twelfth-century runic stone, duplicate only, as the real one is in the National Museum, Edinburgh.

33. The Castle Chapel, Kisimul, Castle Bay

Reached by a Scottish Heritage boat from Castlebay Harbour, this little castle has a so-called chapel against the north-west wall. There are some MacNeil tombs here and a very impressive MacNeil coat of arms.

The castle occupies all of a rocky island a few hundred yards from the harbour. Check the time of the return boat when you arrive. It dates from the fourteenth century. The MacNeils of Barra, originally an Irish family, were involved in piracy in the seventeenth century and in 1838 the owner of the castle, General MacNeil, went bankrupt and sold it to Colonel Gordon of Cluny, one of the landowners involved in sending islanders abroad. However, in 1937 the MacNeils purchased it back, repaired it (roofs were missing and the curtain wall had a large hole) and later, in 2000, leased it to Historic Scotland. It is now open from April to September, from 9.30am to 6.30pm, the last crossing being at 1745 – not an easy number to forget in Scotland.

The chapel (first building on the right as you enter via the yett) is a long, low building, badly lit. It was probably some kind of guard house, but it now has an altar and sundry tombs of the MacNeil family. Above the altar is the family coat of arms. There are two prayer stools and an aumbrey but no sign of the chapel being used, though no doubt there could be a family funeral here.

Compton MacKenzie's Tombstone, Barra

Originally a tower house, the castle has a hall with some weapons (including muskets said to have come from Culloden), the Tanist House (for the heir) which is furnished as a home, the Gorman's House, for the watchman, and the tower which has first and second floors plus a parapet. At some time an addition blocked the postern gate. The castle would have been unable to defend itself from attacking ships, but soldiers inside could no doubt defend themselves from a raiding party.

The name 'Kisimul' means 'Rock of the small bay' but MacGibbon & Ross spell it 'Kismull' which may have another meaning – 'island head' perhaps.

34. Our Lady of the Waves & St John, Vatersay (Roman Catholic)

The way to find this church is: after you cross to Vatersay Island keep right and follow the road round until there is a left fork that reaches this small church. It is bright and cheerful inside, 33ft x 23ft, with a new wooden font and an altar cloth depicting the bread and wine. It is the most southerly Hebridean island church, although Mingulay has a ruined one near its schoolhouse.

Kisimul Castle, Barra, from the north-west. *MacGibbon & Ross, 1889, Vol. III*

Our Lady of the Waves, Vatersay

IONA

The island is reached by a passenger ferry from Fionnphort in Mull (cars are not allowed). For the sake of this book we ignore the abbey, but are concerned with four other buildings.

35. Iona Parish Church

This church was built in 1828 to Telford's standard Parliamentary design by William Thomson. It was re-ordered in 1939 with a pine screen and four central arches at the north end to create a vestry. There is a plain bowl font, and the original tall pulpit (like that on St Kilda) has been removed to the Folk Museum in Kingussie. The original drawings of this building and the manse next door (now a Heritage Centre) are on the wall and the building is open to visitors, there being a 12 o'clock service on Sundays run by a visiting minister from Mull.

36. St Oran's Chapel

Walking on from the church, the next building on the right of the path is St Oran's Chapel. This is tiny, 19ft x 45ft, and was re-roofed in the 1970s. It is basically a mortuary chapel, *c.*1164, as it stands in the burial ground of the kings and princes of Scotland. Note the green man in the arch and the altar dating from 1957. See the picture on the back cover.

37. St Columba's Shrine

At the front of the abbey and to the left of the front entrance is St Columba's Shrine.

This is the smallest building on the island and probably the smallest of any church building in Scotland. The doorway is like a large keyhole, late ninth century according to Pevsner, with barely room for two people inside.

Much good work by MacGregor Chalmers and Lindsey have incorporated it into the actual abbey wall. Inside the main abbey entrance there are steps to the left and a small cell with a seat at the top for a monk to look out for visitors during the daylight hours. This little chapel has a wonderful atmosphere and can be missed by tourists.

Round the back of the abbey and facing the little museum of gravestones is:

38. St Michael's Chapel (Roman Catholic)

Like the Scots Kirk on Canna, this building is like a university chapel so that one half of the congregation faces the other. It is also orientated east-west, unlike the abbey. Dating from the late twelfth or early thirteenth century, it seats about 30 people and has some plain timber boarding, a wonderful timber barrel ceiling – rather like an upturned rowing boat – and of all the buildings on Iona it is my favourite. It is used every Sunday in summer for a 9.30am Mass by the Roman Catholics. The casual visitor should make a point of finding it as it seems forgotten by most tourists.

St Oran's Chapel, Iona. *Wikipedia Commons*

THOMAS TELFORD AND THE PARLIAMENTARY CHURCH

In 1823 in the English Parliament an act was passed 'for Building Additional Places of Worship in the Scottish Highlands and Islands', and funds were given for a standard church and manse at 40 different sites. The well-known bridge and road designer and architect Thomas Telford was put in charge and his designs were used for what is called the 'Parliamentary Church'.

Iona is a very good example, although the church was built by William Thomson using Telford's design. The actual architect's drawings are hanging up inside the building. They usually have two doors on the main face and three or four vertical round-headed windows. Other designers followed the idea so there are newer churches than the Parliamentary varieties.

The General Assembly set up a committee in 1828 to inquire into the 'adequacy of church accommodation' especially in urban areas. It was chaired by Dr Thomas Chalmers, Moderator, in 1832.

ORKNEY

There are numerous ruined churches in Orkney and one or two large buildings like St Peter, Sandwick, which has recently been repaired and is open to the public. It is used for weddings and funerals and is conveniently close to Skara Brae so tourists can easily reach it.

However, only four Orkney churches qualify for this book. They are:

39. Chapel of St Colm & St Margaret, Melsetter, Hoy

To reach this chapel and Melsetter House, take the ferry to Hoy. Remember to phone in advance (01856 791352) to check opening times. Thursday and Sunday afternoons in summer are best.

Melsetter House was designed by W.R. Lethaby, the Arts and Crafts architect in 1898 for the bicycle-seat manufacturer Thomas Middlemore and his weaver wife Theodosia. They were William Morris enthusiasts. On the three gables of what was once a Georgian building he has the letters 'TMT' with '18' on the left-hand gable and '88' on the right-hand one.

The chapel was one of his first experiments with concrete and rubble walls with Caithness slab tiles. There is a pointed vault inside and a bridge-like arch between the nave and sanctuary. The altar is cubic stone and the font cylindrical with a wave pattern on the outside. The stained glass is by Christopher Whall (south wall), William Morris (north window) and the east window a Nativity scene designed by Ford Madox Brown. The crucifixion design on the other Morris window is by Burne-Jones. Lethaby was inspired when designing this chapel by the close union between church and ship, citing Hebrews 6:19, 'we have this hope: a sure and steadfast anchor of the soul'. Maybe this was also the inspiration for Richardson's church at Eriskay (see page 64).

For Lethaby enthusiasts I recommend a trip to Herefordshire to see the unusual thatched Arts and Crafts church at Brockhampton-by-Ross, where the same style prevails. Only this week (November 2009) the local paper has a picture of it showing a Japanese replica, ¾-scale on the twenty-first floor of a large hotel in Osaka. It is used for weddings at £8,000 a time, compared with in the original church here in Herefordshire which only costs £400. It took four months to build and can accommodate up to 60 guests.

40. Italian Chapel, Lamb Holm (Roman Catholic)

On Scapa Flow, Lamb Holm was the site of an Italian POW camp. Following the sinking of HMS *Royal Oak* in 1939 by Gunther Prien in U-47, the Italians were put to work by Churchill's government to build barriers between the mainland and the string of small islands down to South Ronaldsay. The prisoners, encouraged by their priest and presumably by Colonel T.P. Buckland the commandant, set to and built their own chapel. Fortunately, Domenico Chiocetti was an experienced artist, inspired to carry out this work. To help him in the camp were Palumbi, an ironsmith, Buttapesta, cement worker, Primavera and Micheloni, electricians, and several other skilled workers. Two Nissen huts were joined together in 1943 and the sanctuary enclosed by a metal screen. Scrap metal was used, curtains came from Exeter paid for by the prisoners' welfare fund, candelabra were made, and wood from a wrecked ship was used for the tabernacle. The Virgin Mary and Child, surrounded by six angels, was painted by Chiocetti who returned in 1960 to finish off his work. He died in 1999 and a Requiem Mass was held in the chapel attended by islanders and his family. The Mass was taken by Bishop Conti. Today, there is an 11.00am service between April and September on the first Sunday of the month. Apart from two small benches there seem to be no seats but maybe someone hides them in a cupboard.

The chapel is open at all times and is run by a Chapel Preservation Committee. It is kept in remarkably good condition.

41. St Boniface, Papa Westray (Church of Scotland)

To reach this island, take the small aeroplane from Kirkwall (Logan Air). It lands at Westray and then goes on after a few minutes to the smaller island, where passengers get a certificate to say they have been on the shortest commercial flight on any airline, scarcely a mile. By sea it is one and a half hours by ferry to Westray, then a bus ride of half an hour to the ferry terminal to Papa Westray. No cars are taken on the ferry, so a bus or bicycle (one lady was hitching) is still needed to get to the church which is close to the Knap of Howar – the island's answer to Skara Brae, only better, as you are allowed inside this 3000 BC farmstead.

The hog-back tomb at St Boniface, Papa Westray, Orkney

The little church stands in a walled churchyard that contains a ridged hog-back tomb. Dating from the twelfth century, the church has recently been restored by the late Laura Grimond and others. It was given a new roof and is now used once a week in the summer. On our visit, our guide's wife played the accordion (located in a box under the large pulpit on the south wall). There are two box pews with tables (for the squire's meal perhaps) and a gallery with a stack of 20 chairs in case the congregation expands. Benches line the walls and Jim the guide said the niche opposite the pulpit was used to put the unfortunate sinner in (often a girl who had a child out of wedlock) so that she could be harangued by the minister. A book of 'sinners' and their punishments has come to light in a manse in Skye so this must have been a fairly common island practice in Victorian times.

Who was St Boniface? He was a Devon monk (*c*.AD 675-754) who worked mainly in Germany. Gregory II sent him out to preach the gospel in Bavaria and Hesse. While there, he cut down a sacred pagan tree and as the pagans failed to either punish him or to save the tree, many converted to Christianity. However, when he was nearly 80, some pagans attacked and

St Boniface, Papa Westray, Orkney

killed him on the River Borne, near Dokkum. He is buried at Fulda and his feast day is 5 June. There cannot be many Church of Scotland buildings dedicated to a Roman Catholic monk. This little church is well worth a visit. It once had a chancel but this was taken down many years ago and the space used as a burial plot for the Traill family, owners of the island. They disliked the minister at one time and refused to let him disembark on their land (he came by boat from Westray) so the man had to walk along the beach for about three miles to reach the church. In the rain, watch out – the stone steps to the gallery can be slippery and there is no hand rail.

42. St Mary's, Stromness (Scottish Episcopal)

Church Road is almost a wynd, it is so narrow and the church in it is now the Town Hall. However, just beyond this building is a gable end and a locked door, which is St Mary's Episcopal Church, although the building (1888) was not originally a church, possibly a hall.

Amber taking communion, St Mary's, Stromness

It has two Victorian stained-glass windows, but it is not the building that makes this church of interest: it is those who attend the services. Rev Ingrid Cosby, the minister, has a guide dog, Amber, a large labrador-retriever. She attends Holy Communion, comes up to the altar last, puts her front paws on the kneeler board, waits to be blessed and returns to her place. Many of the congregation are disabled – two registered blind – and the local care home is visited with the newly acquired 'sick call communion set'. On Sundays everyone has a special task and on Thursdays there is usually a Holy Communion with intercessions.

This is a little church that has a great heart. Long may it continue. To see it, if locked, phone the number on the board outside.

SHETLAND ISLES

There are two churches I have visited in Shetland that are of interest to visitors for very different reasons:

43. St Margaret, Lunna (Church of Scotland)

On the East Mainland of Shetland, Lunna consists of a large house with red window frames on the hill and a small church below. The church is whitewashed with a red door in the end gable and some buttresses on the east side, a strange series of pilasters roofed over the red door[1] and a forestair on the south gable for approach to the gallery. The church is dated 1753 and has a squint for lepers, except that there is no history of lepers being here.

The church and house are famous as the Second World War headquarters of the Shetland Bus. This was a series of fishing boats that sailed to Norway from Lunna Voe with agents, ammunition and supplies for the Norwegian Resistance. On the return journey, they brought back refugees or agents, some of them in need of medical help, others to be trained and returned.

In the graveyard at Lunna are tombs to some of the Shetland Bus skippers. The whole episode can be investigated further by reading David Howarth's *The Shetland Bus*. David was the Deputy Commander of Lunna House and later in Scalloway, so he writes with authority. The United States Navy supplied three sub-chasers for this enterprise, one of which, *Hirta*, has been restored and can still be seen on occasions in Scalloway.

Notes
1 I note John Hume mentions they could have been built as part of a heating system.

44. Methodist Church, Haroldswick, Unst

This is a new church on Shetland's most northerly island. We called in there after seeing Muckle Flugga, Britain's most northerly lighthouse (now

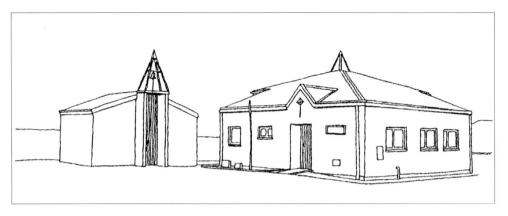

Methodist Church, Haroldswick, Unst. *Courtesy of John Hume*

automatic). On a rock nearby once stood Lady Franklin praying for her husband's safe return, in vain alas, when his Arctic Expedition had vanished.

The church was designed by David Robertson based on a stave church from Norway with wooden panelling (1993) and a separate bell tower. The interior is bright and cheerful with chairs and an altar set across one corner. The place seems always open and we were welcomed with a cup of tea made in the large kitchen. This architect could give some lessons to the Church of England on how to design a community building which has all the requirements and facilities for meetings of most kinds whilst retaining a sense of religious sanctity. Services are held every Sunday at 10.45am or 2.45pm (alternate Sundays). If it was Fair Isle they would share with another church and save on flower-arranging, cleaning and give their congregation some variety.

Two ferries need to be taken to reach Haroldswick from the mainland. Firstly, the Toft-Ulsta ferry, then at the top north-east side of Yell the Gutcher-Blemont ferry. Both are fast, modern ships but timetables need to be studied at the Shetland Island Council transport office in Lerwick or at the Viking Bus Station. The ferries need to be pre-booked for vehicles in summer months (01957 722259).

ST KILDA

44. Christ Church, St Kilda (Non-Denominational)

First of all, St Kilda is not a real saint, but the name 'Kilda' seems to have come from the Norse *Skildir* meaning 'shield'. The islands of St Kilda are Dun and Hirta (where the village is), Soay (famous for its sheep) and Boreray. There are also three main stacs, home to thousands of gannets: Stac Lee, Stac Levenish and Stac an Armin.

The islands were inhabited for hundreds of years. Martin Martin reported that in 1697 there were 160 inhabitants, but in 1930, when the island was evacuated, there were only 36 inhabitants left due to emigration and illness. There were not enough to man the island boats and all were evacuated – the men set to work with the Forestry Commission at Lochaline. Most had never seen a tree before.

The first church dated from the eighteenth century when a number of missionaries sent by SSPCK (the Scottish Society for Promoting Christian Knowledge) went to the island to see to the islanders' spiritual needs. Finally, Rev John Macdonald set up a strict Calvinist religion there with no work permitted on Sundays. He was followed by Rev MacKenzie in 1830 who built the church with its little schoolroom attached at right angles. The building was shelled by a U-boat in the First World War – the people took to their caves and cleits (stone storage hovels) so no humans were killed (merely one sheep) – but it has been restored by the British Army with great care. There is a large pulpit, brought from another island, and sermons lasted for hours on a Sunday. It was often cold and when a stove arrived the minister's housekeeper pronounced it 'Godless like the organ' so it was returned to the ship that had brought it and to the donor. Near the church is the manse, rather a nondescript building, unlike the factor's house which is smart and well looked after. There are occasional services run by the National Trust for Scotland and the civil servants who work on the island, and in summer the volunteers and archaeologists, make up the numbers with some yachtsmen.

St Kilda Schoolhouse bell and church from the west. *Courtesy of Bill Lawson*

The benches (originally just nine of them holding four thin people each) have been rebuilt and there is a monument to the men killed in three wartime crashes, the worst of which was a Sunderland flying boat that hit the top of Conachair (1397ft) killing all 12 crew. Visiting the island is not easy – it took me three years (two cancelled cruises) to get there and there is no hotel. The best way is to become a volunteer with one of the working parties organised by the National Trust for Scotland. The burial ground is easily found, walled off behind the middle cottage in the village street. It is very small so that quite a number of the graves had to be re-used from time to time. The usual custom was to put up a tall stone with no engraving. The only grave easily read today is that to 'Finlay, only son of Angus Gillies, crofter St Kilda, born 8th January, 1878, and died 22nd January 1898 aged 20 years'. He might well have fallen off a cliff when catching birds.

The little school building, attached to the church, has a large map of Canada, slates on the desks (four combined into one), several bottles of ink and a roll-call sheet on a teacher's high desk. The lettering is very faint, but one child is marked as absent 'drowned' so it must have been a real struggle to survive. Having said that, it seems that two out of the four children from the 1930 school are still alive – one in an old people's home and one, a man from an island family, comes back from time to time and had been a visitor in 2008.

What is the future for St Kilda? The tourists will be keen to keep coming but in the winter it is unsafe to land. Presumably it will be a haven for archaeologists, scientists and others. It would be nice to think that, as the cottages are repaired they could be used to accommodate these overnight folk and that there might be a hostel for others so that some sort of island life can continue.

St Kilda Church was used on one occasion by the Rev MacKenzie for a case of breach of promise. The lady concerned proved her case against the man in front of the elders and the priest. He was fined: 100 fully grown fulmars, 50 young solan geese, a hair rope (valuable for cliff climbing to get fulmars) and a promise to contribute to the dowry of the lady in her next 'engagement'. There was no point in fining him with a sum of money as the community coped well without it and hair ropes were much more valuable.

The only other combined church and school I have looked at in detail is St James, Dalby, on the Isle of Man. Here the school closed in 1932 due to a shortage of pupils. In 1920 it had 31 boys and girls and no doubt the priest took part in their education (see *Discovering the Smallest Churches in England*, The History Press, 2008).

ST KILDA FACTS

The island of Hirta is generally known as St Kilda, but there are other islands and stacs in the group made up as follows:

Hirta	1575 acres. Highest point: Conachair, 1397ft
Soay	244 acres. Highest point: 1225ft
Boreray	189 acres. Highest point: 1245ft
Dun	79 acres. Highest point: 576ft
Stac an Armin	3 acres, 627ft high
Stac Levenish	6 acres, 185ft high
Stac Lee	544ft high

Most of the place names are Norse but some are Gaelic. Soay comes from the Norse *saudhr* meaning 'sheep isle'. Today Hirta is roamed by wild Soay sheep.

Other names on St Kilda are:

Am Plaistair	Place of the splashing
Cambir	Burial place
Gealgo	Short geo or creek
Gob a'Ghaill	Mouth of the rock
Gob na Tarnanach	Mouth of the loud sounds
Mullach Mor	Big summit
Oiseval	Steep sloping hill
Rudh Briste	Wreck point of the breaking
Rudha Ghill	The boy's point
Seilg Geo	Hunting creek
Sgeirnan Sgarbh	Rock of the cormorants
Sgeir Dhomnaill	Donald's rock
Sgeir Mac Righ Lochlaine	Rock of the King of Norway's son
Stac an Armin	Stac of the warrior
Stac Dona	Bad stac
Udraclete	Stony ridge

There is some controversy over the name 'Hirta'. The old name was 'Irte' or 'Hyrt' or 'Hirt' and one Celtic scholar says it means 'death' or 'gloom', but he also says that it may just mean 'H-Tar-Tir' or 'west land'.

THE CATHEDRAL OF THE ISLES (EPISCOPAL)
MILLPORT, ISLE OF CUMBRAE, NORTH AYRSHIRE

To reach this impressive building, take the ferry from Largs (North Ayrshire) which costs about £16 including your car and a return journey. We asked for a ticket but they don't give you one. The Episcopal cathedral is in Millport's Bute Terrace surrounded by trees. It was built by William Butterfield in 1851 for the 6th Earl of Glasgow. With a huge spire and an adjacent college, it looks very large but inside it is small, with barely room for 50 in the main nave, but space for an equal number in the adjoining chapel. There are stained-glass windows by Wailes and Hardman and a fine ring of bells. The cathedral is open daily and visitors are allowed to picnic in its delightful grounds. There is a sung eucharist on Sundays at 11.00am. This building takes some finding and when you get there you may well ask what is it doing in a book of small Scottish churches? The reason is that the nave is very small (about 35ft long), it sits about 50 and the rest of the building is a retreat house, vestry, chapel, and of course a very tall spire. There is a Holt organ built for the Episcopal Church of All Saints in Edinburgh and only installed in 2004, a Lipp grand piano and wonderful acoustics. The day we called, after a journey of 10 minutes on the Largs car ferry, there was a violinist practising hard. We had to walk round him to see the little chapel beyond the altar and the Hardman and William Wailes windows.

All this dates from 1851. The architect was William Butterfield and the man who dreamt it up was George Frederick Boyle, 6th Earl of Glasgow, who saw it as a rival to Iona and thought it could become a theological college for the Scottish Episcopal Church. In 1876 it was consecrated as the Cathedral of the Isles.

There is a bus from the ferry to Millport. When you get to the town take the second turning to the right. The spire can be seen rising above the trees, and the gardens are well looked after. Visitors can wander the grounds and if you are staying on the island there is no doubt a concert to attend. Maybe the mystery violin player will be there in person – I sometimes think it was his ghost we saw and listened to, as he didn't move when I walked past, or was it through, him?

LOTHIAN

The county of Lothian includes East Lothian, West Lothian and Midlothian, the latter made famous by Scott's *Heart of Midlothian* which has a print of Edinburgh's Old Tolbooth on the title page as the heart.

46. St Peter, Linlithgow (Scottish Episcopal)

Squashed in between a hairdresser's and a fish shop, this little church of Byzantine style dating from 1928 was designed by J.W. Todd of Dick, Peddle & Todd as a memorial to Bishop George Walpole, Bishop of Edinburgh.

St Peter was originally called St Mildred, after the bishop's wife. The name was later changed to St Peter. The three-light east window, showing St Margaret, the crucified Christ and St Mildred, was made by Miss Howson, daughter of the Archdeacon of Warrington, in 1928. There is a dome over the nave crossing and an apse with a half-dome inside.

Be careful when trying to photograph it as the High Street here has non-stop traffic. There are services at 9.30am on Sundays with a 6.30pm evensong on the first Sunday of the month. For a key, try 01506 842384.

The ruined Linlithgow Palace is on the other side of the street, further back towards Edinburgh with the parish church, easily spotted as it has a 1964 aluminium crown on top which must have caused a bit of controversy when it was installed.

47. Rosslyn Chapel (St Matthew) Roslin, Midlothian (Scottish Episcopal)

The village of Roslin is a few miles outside Edinburgh on the A701 close to Penicuik. It is really an unfinished chapel of the Earl of Rosslyn (note different spelling) as well as being an active church belonging to the Scottish Episcopal Church with services on Sundays at 10.30am and 4.45pm.

I last visited it in the 1960s when it was damp and rather dilapidated, but that was preferable to August 2009 when I arrived on a Saturday afternoon.

St Peter, Linlithgow

Not only does one have to queue to get in at some price, but if you don't join a guided tour it is difficult to see as a solitary tourist.

However, there is £13 million of work (including a new roof) to carry out and this must be a good way of doing it. Don't take a camera (they are forbidden), an animal or toddlers as the roof walk would not be safe for them.

The building took 40 years to construct and was left incomplete. Founded by Sir William Sinclair and his son, Sir Oliver Sinclair, it suffered with Cromwell's troops under Monk in the Civil War but more recently from damp and crumbling stonework. Entry is by the north door and down the aisle to the Lady Chapel where there stands the famous Apprentice Pillar. The master mason had carved the Mason's Pillar, very fine, but during his absence in Rome (or some foreign part) the apprentice carved an even more striking pillar with eight dragons at the base and from their open mouths wind amazing vines. The jealous master mason struck down the poor apprentice when he saw his handiworks which must have brought all construction to a sudden halt.

The Sinclairs were Earls of Orkney and the dragon idea may have come from Norse mythology as the eight dragons of Neifelheim lie at the base of the Yggdrasil, the giant ash that binds earth, heaven and hell together. Continue downstairs into the Sacristy (crypt) which is about 30ft long and seems unused. Note the 1954 stained glass by Pollen in memory of the 5th earl. The south aisle has a window carved with Indian Maze. On the architrave are carved the Seven Deadly Sins and on the other side the Seven Virtues.

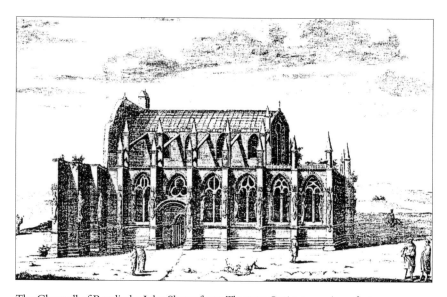

The Chappell of Rosslin by John Slezer, from *Theatrum Scotiae* engraving of 1693

In the Baptistery, you will see some fine 1950 stained glass by W. Wilson. One panel shows St Francis of Assisi and the other a pilot wearing his parachute. This is in memory of PO Peter St Clair Erskine, killed in 1939, and his stepfather, Wg Cdr Sir J. Milbanke, who died in 1947 from injuries sustained during the war. Many visitors miss these windows. There are also some good Clayton and Bell windows (c.1885) and various architects have looked at the structure over the years. Currently it is James Simpson who has the responsibility for getting the building back to normal one day.

Rosslyn has always been a draw for artists and J. Slezer's 1693 engraving is shown here. The local Rosslyn Inn has a plaque stating:

> Here Countless travellers tarried awhile among the distinguished visitors were King Edward VII when Prince of Wales, Dr Samuel Johnson and James Boswell, Robert Burns and Alexander Naysmith, Sir Walter Scott and William and Dorothy Wordsworth.

The castle was painted by Turner, the chapel inside by David Roberts RA (1842) and there is a painting of Sir William St Clair playing golf (1771) by George Chalmers. This can be seen in the current guide book (£4.25), which has been written in a scholarly style by the current earl.

Absent from the guidebook, Roslin village was the scene of an explosion at the explosives factory there in 1916. One building caught fire and three men ran to get the girls out. Two (Morrison and Young) managed this while George Sang kept up a chain of water buckets to damp down the fire. Twelve minutes after the girls were rescued the whole building blew up. Morrison and Sang were members of the Scottish Mountaineering Club. With Young, they were awarded the Edward Medal and the Sang family still possess George's medal today. As a young boy I recall being driven fast by Morrison in his open tourer to grandmother's house in Edinburgh where the medal was pinned to grandfather's portrait on the wall.

Rev Michael Fass, until recently Priest in Charge of Rosslyn Chapel, has given me a copy of his book *Faith and Place* which tells how he was standing in the transept one day, Palm Sunday in fact, when a visitor asked him to move. 'You are standing on the spot where the ley-lines meet and I have come a long way so please move over.'

This was a New-Ager. Rosslyn has featured in many recent publications like *Rosslyn – Guardian of the Secrets of the Holy Grail* and *The Sign and Seal*, many of which are on sale in the bookshop. How, Michael asks, did we get to this situation? It is as if the Glastonbury crowds have moved to Scotland

and singled out Rosslyn as their own centre – or 'center' as many are from the USA. 'I am passionate,' writes Michael, 'that this should be a place not of unhealed or false memories, not of secrets and sensational speculation or "esoteric" enquiry – for there are no secrets here – and not of the New Age search for personal satisfaction, but rather that it should be a place of Healing, Reconciliation and Prayer.'

The Founder, who was neither a Crusader nor a Templar, to seek salvation for his soul, founded a college of ordained and lay clerks to say Masses regularly in this building, which has never been finished but stands in its finery perfectly able to carry out the functions of a collegiate church. The chapel fell into disuse and the Earl of Rosslyn's nearby castle became a ruin. It was Queen Victoria in the 1860s, who liked ruins, who instructed the earl to re-open his chapel for Anglican worship and in a solemn service it was re-dedicated to the Scottish Episcopal Church, which is appropriate as it was originally a Catholic chapel. For those of you horrified by the tourist invasion, Michael says we 'should not unduly focus on "financial" aims which are, of course, a means to an end, but not the end in itself; that here we do not boast of earthly rule or power or achievement in politics or science or knowledge, but rather we acknowledge the loving reality of the Incarnation of Jesus Christ in our lives.'

MORAY

North of Aberdeen, Morayshire has several interesting churches. For more information, see Howat and Seton, *Churches of Moray*, 1981.

48. Our Lady of Perpetual Succour, Chapeltown (Roman Catholic)

This is a well-hidden church. To find it, take the A939 going north and turn off at Tomintoul on the B9008 to Knockandhu where you turn off on a minor road to the Braes of Glenlivet. The church is suddenly in front of you and a cottage on the right supplies the key.

The reason for the remoteness of this chapel is that it was first established in 1712 when a Catholic seminary was set up at Scalan, which later became Blairs College. 1712 was not a year when Catholics, usually Jacobites, could easily practice their religion.

Father Mackenzie contacted John Kinross (the author's grandfather and namesake), then the architect for the Marquis of Bute, to draw up a plan. The result is probably his best church building in Scotland, certainly as an interior. Externally, the tower over the entrance door at the west end and a crow-stopped gable are Norman Scottish, although the local paper said it was 'in a style of architecture common to Brittany'. It is built of red granite and cream-coloured limestone, with a roof and floor of local red wood. The wall boards are painted salmon pink and the ceiling is barrel-shaped with cross beams underneath. Around the top of the walls is the Lord's Prayer in Latin as well as numerous heraldic shields. There is a finely carved altar rail and a canopied reredos which were gifted by Father Mackenzie to his congregation. Finally a Belgian firm was called in to carry out the gilded stations of the cross.

The lighting was by brass lamps suspended from the ceiling. A carved oak bishop's chair and an oak pulpit sitting on white Elgin sandstone completes the picture. The chapel is attached to a small flat for the Father, but it is not clear if he lived here.

Today there is a service every third week sometimes taken by one of the monks from Pluscarden Abbey – worth a visit if you are in the area.

Our Lady of Perpetual Succour, Chapeltown

49. The Michael Kirk, Gordonstoun, Duffus, Elgin (Interdenominational)

This small chapel was built originally as a 1705 mausoleum to Sir Robert Gordon, but when John Kinross was commissioned by Lady Gordon-Cumming (who lived in the building now used as the school) in June 1900 to turn it into an Episcopal chapel for the use of her family, he had to start from scratch as only an unroofed shell remained.

Interior of The Michael Kirk, Gordonstoun, 1901. Note the Gordon monument on the left, and John Kinross' statue of St Michael in the reredos. He was very pleased with this!

A heavy teak door was inserted, amber glass in the Gothic window, and an altar at the east end which was given a raised floor. Black and white marble tiles were laid and a harmonium installed. No heating or lighting was inserted (quite normal at this period) as Lady Gordon-Cumming was usually only a summer resident in her home. The carved reredos of St Michael and the Dragon was removed. After woodworm treatment, it was put back in the corner. Our family are especially keen on light in buildings and as the chapel has to rely on window light maybe the reredos blocked the window and a compromise was taken.

Oak panelling was inserted by Scott Morton to Kinross's design, and bench seating for 50 people. Eight months after completion, the chapel was used for the baptism of the Gordon-Cumming's third son, Michael Willoughby.

Today the chapel is used by the school every Sunday for an 8.40am communion and a candle-lit compline at 9.00pm. It is too small for the entire school but at least it is not used as a library or, as someone told me, a tuck shop. For those calling at term time, it would be best to contact the chaplain, but in the holidays the key is kept in the school office.

Mark Piper, the principal at Gordonstoun School, has written the following paragraphs about The Michael Kirk:

> The Michael Kirk itself – and the kirkyard – represent life's journey or cycle. Babies are christened there, young people (several former members of Gordonstoun each year) marry here, many who are part of the Gordonstoun community wish to rest there when there time on earth is done. In the shadow of a six hundred year old stone cross and under the kindly influence of a modern school, life bursts into bud, bears fruit and withers away. No demands are made on us, no threats hang over us, we are simply invited to be there and be ourselves there.
>
> Thus the Michael Kirk has become for generations of Gordonstoun students and those who guide them a place of anticipation, thoughtfulness and prayer. As a chapel, its atmosphere is unique and, when outside, at any season of the year, one is nearer God's heart in this particular garden than anywhere else on earth.

Henry Brereton, former Warden of Gordonstoun, has written about the second Sir Robert Gordon, known as the 'Wizard', whose widow built the mausoleum that became The Michael Kirk.

Born in 1647, Robert was a studious boy and his father sent him to the University of Padua, where he became a scientist, much taken with experiments. On his return to Scotland he married firstly Margaret Forbes, daughter of William, 11th Lord Forbes. She died in childbirth two years after their marriage so he married again to Elizabeth Dunbar of Caithness.

She inherited a fortune from her father and some of this money went to building the mausoleum.

Robert set up a laboratory on the ground floor of Gordonstoun House and the locals soon gave him the name of Wizard as the bangs and flares at night were consistent with a seventeenth-century scientist at work.

Brereton, however, recounts the legend of Robert's fight with the Devil which started in Padua. One student had dressed up as the Devil's priest and chanted the Mass backwards. A man gets up and says, 'Well, gentlemen, you have summoned me, what can I do for you?'

The answer is, 'We would learn the secrets of the universe that the King of Heaven has denied'.

'Well,' says the Devil, 'I am ready to do this but there is a price'.

'What is the price?' asks the student-priest.

The Michael Kirk, Gordonstoun, today. Built on the site of Ogstoun church as a memorial to Sir Robert Gordon (1649-1704), known as the 'Wizard Lord'

'A human soul', answers the Devil.

Robert then asks, 'Do you give credit?' The Devil says that he will submit a bill 12 months from this day exactly.

One year later he meets the Devil who says he has come for payment. 'Take that shadow there,' he says, pointing to his shadow next to that of the Devil. Soon there is only one left and the Devil says he will come at Halloween and collect him. Back in Scotland he builds a magic circle for his new stable block, known as the Round Square, to keep out the Devil. On Halloween night Robert invites the parson of Duffus to come and spend an evening with him at Gordonstoun. The two men drink whisky while Robert tells of his fight with the Devil. There is a storm brewing. A gust of wind blows in a window and the tapestry moves. Beneath it appears a cloven hoof. 'Your hour has come,' says the Devil.

'Ah, but I put the clock back one hour,' says Robert.

'I will claim your immortal soul in an hour,' says the Devil and the rain vanishes.

The vicar comes to his senses and asks Robert what he will do next. 'Go into my Round Square for I am immune from him there'. The parson says he must make for Birnie Church which will be safer.

Now the minister of Birnie, Rev John McKean, was returning home late. Suddenly a running man overtook him, saying, 'Am I on the road to Birnie Kirk?'

'Why, yes, Laird,' says McKean, recognising Robert, 'Straight on'.

A few minutes after, a rider on horseback with two hounds stopped and asked McKean if he had seen a man pass. 'No, not a soul', said McKean – realising this was no ordinary man and that the Laird was in danger. There was no further noise and McKean now walked only on grass so that he could hear the sounds in the night. There was a mighty scream! He stopped under a tree and the rider returned, a body on his saddle with the fangs of a hound on its throat.

Next morning they found Robert in a ditch, his throat torn by a wild animal.

Sir Walter Scott heard the tale, for in *The Lay of the Last Minstrel*, he writes:

He learned the art that none may name
In Padua, far beyond the sea;
Men said he changed his mortal frame
By feat of magic mystery.
For when in studious mood he paced
St Andrews cloistered Hall

His form no darkening shadow traced
Upon the sunny wall.

Strangely, the story is still told today, though it is known that in 1704 the Laird died in his bed; John McKean is supposed to have died in June of that year, the Laird in September.

Boys are often frightened of going out at night, especially on Halloween. Brereton recalls that in 1951 a notable Frenchman, Antonin Besse, founder of St Anthony's College, Oxford, died while on a visit to Gordonstoun. The French Consul had to be called from Edinburgh and the body was examined by flickering candlelight in The Michael Kirk, so the Consul could give permission for it to be flown to Perpignan. Brereton helped undo the coffin and seal it up again. Instead of being frightened that maybe the Devil was watching them, he said the building was quiet, warm and very peaceful, for even the tomb of Sir Robert looking on did not produce any bad feelings. Maybe the Wizard was laid to rest at long last.

Michael Kirk Graveyard

In the graveyard are the tombs of the family. There is a Celtic cross to Lady Florence Josephine Gordon-Cumming, who died in Pitmilly, Fife, in 1922. She commissioned John Kinross (the author's grandfather and namesake) to build the chapel. Her husband outlived her by eight years and died in 1930. His name appears on the step of the tomb. Nine years later, Alexander, fifth Baronet, who had won the Military Cross in the First World War with the Cameron Highlanders, was buried nearby. Sir William's second son, Roualeyn, who fought at Jutland, and died at the early age of 32, has a memorial close to his family.

There are some school monuments, including one to Cecilia Napier, Mr Brereton's secretary for 20 years. She died in 1967. Strangely, the author's school secretary, also called Napier, died at about the same time. There is a sad monument to Ian Mark Ruscoe, a climber who unroped on Ben Nevis in the snow and fell to his death. His daughter was born three months later; he was only 29.

There are several graves of local people, including quite a number of the Mustard family. One tomb is to a road contractor and there are a few seamen. Of the modern graves, there is one to Anthony Norman Jones, House Master of the Round Square, who died suddenly in his house on 17 July 1980, aged 46.

TIN CHURCHES

There are several tin churches in Scotland, some like Dalswinton are quite large. They are in Ian Smith's useful book *Tin Tabernacles*, Central Books, 2004. I have listed below ones that are included in the book. One has moved and is now a woodwork shed on the hill above the village of Dull. As it is painted an interesting shade of green, maybe the village should change its name.

Dalswinton, Dumfries & Galloway (Church of Scotland)
St Fillans, Killin, Stirlingshire (Episcopal & Roman Catholic)
Strathnaver, Syre, Sutherland (Church of Scotland)
Tomatin, Inverness-shire (Church of Scotland)

Most of these were constructed by Spiers of Glasgow and shipped by rail, and then horse and cart, to be erected on site. Local builders were employed, probably supervised by a man from the firm. Other suppliers, south of the border, were Dixon of Liverpool and Humphreys of Knightsbridge in London. Some have changed use by now and become village halls, schools, one is a shop (Fort Augustus) and a few are derelict. In Victorian times a flat-pack church would cost £77 10s (30ft x 20ft with a 16ft ridge), or erected on site for a total of £107 10s. My prices are taken from an advertisement of Coopers of Old Kent Road, London. Another supplier in the Midlands was Boulton & Paul, who during the Second World War made aeroplanes including the *Defiant* fighter.

They could be purchased from catalogues and sent by train to be erected by local builders. It is a credit to their construction that so many still exist and are in use today.

PERTH & KINROSS

The two old counties are now one and are popular with weekenders from Edinburgh and other places. There are several churches worth a visit.

Using Pitlochry as a base there are three small churches to see to the north and two to the south. It probably doesn't pay to visit them on a Sunday as two had services when we called, one was open and one was recovering from a wedding the day before.

50. St Adamnan, Kilmaveonaig, Blair Atholl, Perthshire (Scottish Episcopal)

This small church is clearly seen from the Pitlochry-Blair Atholl road and the key can be obtained from the Tilt Hotel opposite. It was an old church rebuilt in 1794 by John Stewart with three bays and a ball-finialled birdcage bellcote on the west gable. In 1890, Rev Sugden added a vestry with battlements at the west end with a horseshoe-shaped doorway that doesn't match the three round-arched lights in the south wall. Inside there are pink walls with timber panelling in both nave and chancel, a 1912 wooden reredos by Lorimer that partly obscures the east window and an enormous hatchment to James Robertson of Lude (d.1803) with a smaller one to his wife Margaret on the south wall. There is a west gallery and a nice two-light window of 1925 to St Euan (the same person as St Adamnan) and St Bride.

The lychgate dates from 1901 and the whole building and graveyard seem well looked after. There is a service every Sunday at 10.00am with a 6.30pm evensong in summer.

51. St Anne, Dowally (Church of Scotland)

Very close to the busy A9 this is an 1818 rubble T-shaped church with a new 1985 porch. The north gallery was removed in 1907 and there is some panelling that used to be in Dunkeld Cathedral. There is some modern stained glass by James Ballantine II.

St Adamnan, Kilmaveonaig. *Courtesy of Alison Poole*

52. Fortinghall, Parish Church (Church of Scotland)

Carrying on towards Aberfeldy on the B846, turn left to Fortinghall. The church is next to the inn and most of the village dates from 1901/2. It was Sir Donald Currie who employed Dunn and Watson to rebuild the church and much of the village. Crowstepped gables with a birdcage bellcote, a semi-tunnel-vaulted roof and much oak panelling make this a church worth a visit. There are some ninth-century stones on the sills, a bell from Rotterdam (1765) as well as a seventh-century handbell. One of them was probably a passing bell as at Linton (see page 32). When we called there were many ladies admiring the flowers from the previous day's wedding.

There are two other reasons for including this church, which some may think too large for listing. It has the oldest yew tree in Scotland outside, supposedly 3000 years old, and there is also a rumour that it was planted by the father of Pontius Pilate, who was reputedly born here when his father was serving in the Roman Army.

Near the yew tree is the grave of Rev Duncan Macara who brought 'order and tranquility after the Jacobite wars'. Part of the yew tree had to be walled back so that his tombstone could be seen.

At the east end of the church is a monument to one of the Campbells of Glen Lyon, the family involved in the Glencoe Massacre of 1692. On the way home we passed the village of Dull. This may sound unexciting but it has been considerably brightened by the erection of a green former tin church (see the section on Tin Churches, page 96) from the backstreets of Aberfeldy. It is now used as a workshop.

53. Holy Trinity, Pitlochry (Scottish Episcopal)

This church is easily passed without realising that it is open on occasions (see its noticeboard) and that it has a wonderful painted reredos by Sir Ninian Comper, glass by Kempe (1906) and an organ by Hele & Co. Other glass is by Hardman of Birmingham, Ballantine & Co., and there is a 1956 three-light west window by Alex Russell in modernist style. There is a scissor-truss roof in both nave and chancel, but it is the black, red and gold reredos which is that seeing, as well as the large tunnel-vaulted 1923 porch and the fast stream that flows through the churchyard. If you have trouble finding it open, phone 01796 472176.

Holy Trinity, Pitlochry, Espiscopal

In the churchyard is the grave of Sir Robert Watson-Watt, founder of radar, who died in 1973. A tourist was placing a flower by his tomb when I arrived and one hopes that the tomb will be placed on the map, as although Pilochry is not short of visitors, few come here.

The architect was Buckeridge of Oxford and many consider he has placed an English village church in a Scottish town, but few English villages have such a wealth of decoration. Pitlochry has many hotels and other places to stay as well as a lively theatre. We used it as our main base for seeing Scottish churches.

54. Foss Kirk (Church of Scotland)

Proceeding from Tenandry as far as Tummel Bridge at the end of Loch Tummel, cross the bridge and turn left to the other bank of the loch. When we did this a baby red squirrel ran across the road, only the second I have ever seen, so Foss, which appears very soon with its nearby cottage, is very rural. Inside is a large pulpit and monuments to the Menzies family, one of

Foss Kirk, Interior

whom was killed in the First World War. There was a faded bowl of sweet peas when we called and one wondered how often this church is used. There is a stone boulder stoup stuck in the front wall that is probably medieval.

55. Morenish Chapel (Church of Scotland)

Roughly the same date as Lethaby's Hoy chapel, this stands on the north bank of Loch Tay between Killin and Kenmare. It was built by Joseph (later Sir Joseph) and Aline White Todd in memory of their daughter Elvira. It has a central Tiffany window in the east depicting the 10 commandments and upper roundels showing scenes from the Bible. The entrance, round-headed, has Art Nouveau-style hinges with the Todds' initials and the date 1902. In the north side there is a fireplace with green-tiled ingoes and an oak overmantel. Two bronze sarcophagi dated 1924 and 1926 commemorate Sir Joseph and Aline.

In spite of all this lavish decoration, the church is used on the first Sunday in the month for a 3.00pm service in the summer.

56. Tenandry Kirk (Church of Scotland)

North of Pitlochry across the Tummel Bridge and first right; the church here has no car park. Originally a chapel of ease built in 1835, this is an L-shaped building with galleries at north and south. The pulpit is on the west side. One of the families who are associated with this church are the Campbells of Urrard House (one of whom was killed in Malaya, 1951) and on whose land was fought the Battle of Killiekrankie, 1689. More details of this can be seen at the National Trust for Scotland Centre nearby.

Tenandry Kirk

STIRLINGSHIRE

The county of Stirlingshire is well placed in central Scotland and the city has much to see, especially the castle, old bridge and the Wallace monument.

57. Scottish Churches House Chapel, Dunblane, Stirling (Interdenominational)

Immediately opposite the cathedral in Kirk Street is the retreat house used for conferences and meetings. No-one knew about the chapel until 1961 when it was uncovered during some restoration work. It has a fine barrel-vaulted roof, two aumbries and a free-standing oak cross. There is some bench seating and the small holy place has been tastefully restored by Honeyman, Jack and Robertson. It is supposed to date from the thirteenth century and is used by those attending courses here, whatever their religion. The daily service is at 9.00am and the building is open all the year at normal working hours.

58. St Fillans (Tin) Church, Killin (Scottish Episcopal)

A delightful green-roofed, white-walled Scottish Episcopal church in Killin's main street, this tin building was built by Spiers of Glasgow and erected in 1876. Inside it is finished in pine. There is a service at 10.30 of Holy Communion on Sunday mornings and a Roman Catholic Mass at 2.30 on Sunday afternoons.

THE STRACHAN BROTHERS AND THEIR STAINED GLASS

St Margaret's Chapel in Edinburgh Castle has some wonderful stained glass (see page 42) which, like the Robert Lorimer designed National War Memorial next door, is by Douglas Strachan. Born in 1875 in Aberdeen, he went to Gray's School of Art and then moved to London where he attended the Royal Academy. Returning to Aberdeen, his first church glass was at St Nicholas Church. He was not happy with the result but was persuaded to carry on and, after the First World War, was asked (in 1935) what effect the various modern movements like cubism and futurism had had on his work. 'None' was the answer. 'Such an understanding is best left to others … I have never regarded, compared or weighed my own works in relation to anything but the image in my head, and the most effective means I could contrive for giving satisfaction to it.'

Fine examples of his work can be seen at Hyndland Church, Glasgow and Trinity Church, St Andrews, as well as the great east window at Paisley Abbey.

His brother, Alexander, who was his more-famous brother's assistant, was not so prolific. His work can be seen at St Fillans Church, Aberdour (1930), and is usually on a smaller scale than that of Douglas. They are very highly coloured and the brothers' work can sometimes be confused. Priestfield Parish Church in Edinburgh has a war memorial window by Alexander and his two assistants, Mary Wood and Douglas Hamilton (1921), and Mary Wood also designed a window to St Aidan at St Cuthbert's, Edinburgh (1928).

In his interesting book *Scotland's Stained Glass*, Michael Donnelly shows how Scotland's glass developed not only in churches but in municipal and other buildings as well. Some can be seen at the Ely Cathedral Stained Glass Museum and at Glasgow's Burrell Collection. Two fine examples of modern glass he illustrates are Susan Laidler's 'The Forest' at St John's Church, Bath Street, Glasgow (1986) and the Robert Burns Memorial Window at Alloway Parish Church, Ayrshire (1996).

Work by non-Scots stained-glass designers can be seen in various churches in Scotland. For example: Harry Clarke (Ireland) at Notre Dame Convent, Bearsden; Louis Davis at Dunblane Cathedral and All Saints, St Andrews; Henry Holiday at Dunfermline Abbey, Fife; C.E. Kempe at St Giles Cathedral, Edinburgh; Morris and Burne-Jones at Kirkaldy Old Parish Church, Fife, St Giles, Edinburgh and Kings College Chapel, Aberdeen; Pat Pollen of Dublin at Rosslyn Chapel; Tiffany at St Cuthbert's Parish Church, Edinburgh; and C.W. Whall at Falkirk Parish Church and the Clark Memorial Church, Largs.

APPENDIX I

THE SCOTTISH REDUNDANT CHURCHES TRUST

4 Queen's Gardens
St Andrews
Fife KY16 9TA
Tel: 01334 472032 (contact@srct.org.uk)

The SRCT is a charity limited by guarantee which looks after the following redundant churches:

East Church, Cromarty, Ross-shire
Currently closed due to restoration work

Tibbermore Church, Perth & Kinross
For keyholder, phone 01738 582450

Penholm Kirk, Aberdeenshire
Open July to August, Sundays 1-4.00pm (between Johnshaven and Inverbervie)
Key holder: 01561 361631

Pettinain Church, S. Lanarkshire
Open July to August, Sundays 1-4.00pm. Key holder: 01555 870260

St Peter's Kirk, Sandwick, Orkney
Open April to October, 10am-6pm, November to March. Key holder: 01856 841743

In process of acquisition:

Kildrummy Kirk, Aberdeenshire.

All churches are Church of Scotland and many, like St Peter's, are still used for weddings, funerals and other events. Alas, they are all too large for inclusion in this book.

Above: St Peter's, Sandwick

Left: St Peter's, Sandwick, prior to restoration

APPENDIX II

SCOTLAND'S CHURCHES SCHEME

In 1993, Scotland's Churches Scheme was set up by all denominations to encourage the following six aims and purposes:

1. To promote spiritual understanding by enabling the public to appreciate all buildings in Scotland designed for worship and active as living churches.

2. To advance the education of the public in history, architecture and other environmental subjects through the study of historic church buildings of all denominations in Scotland, their contents and environs.

3. To encourage co-operation among the churches themselves and between them and their local communities.

4. To publish details of churches open to visitors through a handbook, *Churches to Visit in Scotland*, as a guide to visitors and to encourage support for the churches visited through donations, especially for specific appeals.

5. To receive donations for churches, in particular or in general, in order to provide when requested advice on the care and reception of visitors and the provision of historical or other information.

6. To promote the common purpose of mission through the ministry of welcome for visitors, tourists and pilgrims.

This scheme is based at Dunedin, Holehouse Road, Eaglesham, Glasgow G76 0JF and the Director is Dr Brian Fraser. Many of the churches in their guide are in this book, but a good few are not as the handbook gives no indication as to the size of the churches.

APPENDIX III

SCOTTISH CHURCHES ARCHITECTURAL HERITAGE TRUST

15 North Bank Street, Edinburgh EH1 2LP
Telephone: 0131 225 8644
Email: info@schat.org.uk

Chairman: The Lord Penrose
Founder: Magnus Magnusson KBE

This is a Heritage Trust formed in 1978 to care for Scottish church buildings in use by raising funds for their repair and restoration. The Charitable Trust is dependent on support from individuals, business organisations and those concerned with maintaining Scotland's architectural heritage.

Posters, donation forms and information can be obtained from the Director at the postal address, email address and telephone number given above.

Congregations have to raise funds themselves to match the grants and, if there is a time lapse, then the grant is withdrawn and they have to reapply.

Three circular churches have been given grants: Kilmorich Parish Church, Cairndow, Argyll; Glenorchy Parish Church, Dalmally, Argyll; and Kilarrow, Bowmore, Islay. I visited the latter, which is quite large although the actual floor area is tiny as there is so much seating.

The total granted for 2007 was £118,456 and for 2008 £95,200.

The following Scottish churches have been assisted by grants from SCAHT in the last two years – most are too large for this book and only Rosslyn Chapel (which is well organised to get the maximum out of its visitors) appears.

CHURCHES GRANT-AIDED, YEAR ENDING NOVEMBER 2007

Church of Scotland

Athelstaneford Parish Church. Roll 215. Cruciform church of 1870 incorporating the 1583 gable and bellcote of the earlier church. Repairs to bellcote.

Boghall Parish Church. Roll 85. Traditional preaching-box church by William Davidson, 1847, altered 1902. Window repairs. Conditional on external glazing not being fitted.

St Nicholas Buccleuch, Dalkeith. Roll 530. Choir of collegiate church, 1406, with nave and transepts by David Bryce, 1851. Masonry repairs.

St John's Church, Dunoon. Roll 236. Large neo-Gothic church by John Bryden, 1877, with tall spire and many gables. Repairs to spire.

St Margaret's Parish Church, Restalrig, Edinburgh. Roll 426. Fifteenth-century collegiate church rebuilt in Gothic Revival style by William Burn, 1836. General repairs. Grant conditional on supervision by qualified conservation consultant, no damp-proof course, ventilators in windows to be in pulley styles, not at head.

Kilmelford Church, by Oban. Roll 40. T-plan church of 1790 with tall roof, lancet windows and eight-spoke wheel window over entrance. General repairs.

St Nicholas, Lanark. Roll 580. Classical church of 1774 by John Reid in centre of Lanark, on site of earlier church. Repairs to masonry and re-rendering.

Coltness Memorial Church, Newmains. Roll 246. Cathedral-like church, 1878, William Wallace architect, in Norman-Gothic style. General repairs.

Scalloway Church, Shetland. Roll 170. Square stone box with slate roof, 1841. Roof repairs.

Scarista Church. Roll 101. Harled rectangular church with attached porch and vestry, given character by pointed arch windows. Window repairs.

Tillicoultry Parish Church. Roll 825. Neo-Perpendicular church, 1829, William Stirling, with octagonal bell tower overhanging the entrance façade. Roof and window repairs.

Weisdale Kirk. Roll 170. Single-storey harled kirk, with bellcote, 1863. Repairs to floor following outbreak of dry rot.

Scottish Episcopal Church

Rosslyn Chapel, Roslin. Roll 176. Choir of fifteenth-century collegiate church renowned for spectacular stone carving. General repairs.

Roman Catholic Church

St Patrick's Church, Cowgate, Edinburgh. Roll 700. Built as the English Chapel by John Baxter, 1771, re-ordered 1856 when adopted by the Catholic Church. Roof and masonry repairs.

St Teresa of Lisieux, Possil, Glasgow. Roll 2000, attendance 260. T-plan, red-brick church with sandstone dressings, 1956. Alexander McAnally. Repairs to tower and windows.

St Paul, Whiteinch, Glasgow. Roll 1000, attendance 336. Large church of red stone with copper roof, 1950s, by Charles Gray of Sir Reginald Fairly & Partners. Complete set of windows by Gabriel Loire. General repairs.

Clachan Church, Applecross. Multi-denominational. Rectangular stone church of 1817 on a site of immense historic and archaeological significance. Summary conservation report commissioned from Andrew Wright.

Link Christian Fellowship, Dunfermline. Assemblies of God, roll 85. Built as a Masonic Lodge in 1913, by Crawford & Fraser. Powerful Classical design with Doric pilastered street elevation and remarkably intact interior with Ionic columns. General repairs. Summary conservation report commissioned from Stephen Newsom, £1,760 and grant.

Wellsprings Community, Newcraighall, Edinburgh. Non-denominational. Miners' church of polychrome brick, 1877, originally

Church of Scotland, closed 1968 and being brought back into ecclesiastical use. General repairs.

Kirkandrews Kirk, Ecumenical. Miniature fort of 1906 designed by Walter Higgenbottom to enhance the landscape of local landowner James Brown. Masonry repairs.

CHURCHES GRANT-AIDED, YEAR ENDING NOVEMBER 2008

Church of Scotland

Yester Parish Church, Gifford. Significant parish church of the reformed tradition, James Smith, 1710, T-plan in white harl with a square tower topped with a short spire. General repairs including replacing cement render with a lime harl.

Dysart Kirk. Romanesque church of cruciform plan with tower and spire at the crossing. Roof and masonry repairs.

St Andrews, Ayr. Perpendicular Gothic Revival church by John B. Wilson, 1893, distinguished by its tall spire and collection of stained glass. Repairs to church, tower and steeple.

St Mary of Wedale. Stone-built Gothic Revival church, 1878 by Edward Maidman, with tall tower and spire. Dry rot eradication and repairs to gutters and rainwater goods.

Crosshouse Parish Church. Gothic Revival church with pinnacled tower, 1822, by Bruce and Sturrock. Masonry repairs to tower.

Barony St John's, Ardossan. Rectangular church, 1844, by Black & Salmon, with Gothic pinnacles and small clock tower. Window repairs.

St Ninian's Priory Church, Whithorn. White-harled rectangular hall-church of 1822 with later nineteenth-century tower. Roof repairs.

St John's Renfield, Glasgow. Bold and striking church of the late Gothic Revival with modern influences, 1931, by James Taylor Thomson. Repairs to flèche, roof and masonry.

St Ninian's, Bigton, Shetland. Simple stone-built rectangular plan with pitched slate roof and porch. Solution to persistent damp problems sought. Grant towards specialist report by Scottish Lime Centre Trust.

Abercorn Church. Charming country church dating from the eleventh century, with later aisles including 1707 Hopetoun Aisle by William Bruce; rest of interior remodelled by Peter MacGregor Chalmers in 1893. Repairs to roof structure and plaster following woodworm infestation.

St Ninian's and Forglen, Turriff. Originally built in a T-plan, 1794, bellcote added 1875, altered to rectangular church in 1914 by A. Marshall Mackenzie. Repairs to bellcote.

Annan Old Parish Church. Hall-church of 1789 with galleries on three sides; extension to rear and bell tower added 1801. Roof repairs.

Kirkcaldy Old Parish Church. Massive medieval stone tower; the body of the church of 1808 by James Elliot. Masonry repairs to tower.

Polmont Old Parish Church. Romanesque-style church, 1844, by J. Tait, with two towers flanking the entrance; windows by Ballantine. Window repairs.

Belhelvie Parish Church. 1878 by William Smith. Tall stone-built, Gothic-style hall-church with steep slate roof and gabled bellcote. Window repairs.

Greenock West United Reform Church. Perpendicular Gothic design by James Baird, 1839, with pinnacled façade and horseshoe gallery. Repairs to roof and masonry.

Hawick Baptist Church. Masonry repairs required. Grant towards conservation report.

Following are the introductory letter to supporters of the Trust and the *Chairman's Report* for 2009:

Dear Supporter,

We hope you enjoy the enclosed Annual Report. As an individual supporter of SCAHT, you may be interested to see the range of support we offer congregations and the breadth of our support over the whole of Scotland. We have a heavy but wonderful responsibility to ensure the preservation of buildings that are both part of our cultural heritage but also vital cogs in the machinery of a Community.

The amounts granted often belie the level of support actually provided, and we are very fortunate to have a broad-based network of experts covering the Country that we are able to call upon to offer advice at a very preliminary stage of an application. By using this network, and calling upon their expertise, we can very often assure than a final application is appropriate to the actual problem of the building rather than any perceived problem.

We also often find ourselves asked about Funding and are pleased to offer advice on finding the best route to suit the need of the application. Many congregations have to delay important remedial works due to the difficulties of funding, or finding match funding in the present economic climate. It is therefore all the more important that an application is well formulated before it comes in front of Funding Bodies. We feel our work in this area is worthwhile and offers excellent value to those who in turn support us.

As you will appreciate, it is increasingly challenging to find the funds we aim to redistribute annually and therefore your continued support is both essential and very much appreciated.

Please enjoy the Annual Review and I do hope we, and those we support in turn, can continue to benefit from your generosity. We are always happy to discuss our work and welcome any opportunity, so please, as a supporter, we would like you to feel part of the 'team'.

I hope to hear from you again in the future, and once again, many thanks.

With all good wishes
Stuart Beattie
Director

CHAIRMAN'S REPORT

My last Chairman's Report spoke of turbulent times and to some extent 2009 continues this theme. The economic crisis may make fewer headlines but the fall-out from it will be felt for many months yet. I shall return to this but 2009 also saw a significant change to the Scottish Churches Architectural Heritage Trust with the retiral, and too soon afterwards, the sad death of Florence Mackenzie of which you will read more elsewhere in this annual Report.

2009 has been a time of change. We saw changes for those who look after our historic buildings, with the National Trust for Scotland having a torrid time and Historic Scotland looking to make savings. We saw changes in how grant giving bodies set their criteria for giving – a fact that can dramatically impact on our income for redistribution – and we saw changes proposed in the approach to be adopted to the conservation of our ecclesiastical heritage. A report to the Minister in September 2009 pointed out that over 3,500 ecclesiastical buildings are 'listed' with 15% noted as category 'A'. As is often the case, we find ourselves in fairly familiar territory: reductions in funding streams and yet more calls on our resources. The Scottish churches stock gets older every year and the need to take action, sometimes minor sometimes major, becomes more urgent. Work that is delayed because of financial restraint invariably costs more by the time the need becomes a crisis.

The work we all do to maintain our Scottish churches is vital, especially in more rural areas where a church building can be the focus of a community. Iconic churches in city and town centre situations are vital too and very often establish the town centre scene, but often find greater support for that reason, and from their larger congregations. The important element of course is getting the right advice to make an informed decision as regards what may be causing a problem and how best to deal with it.

The Scottish Churches Architectural Heritage Trust aims to become more active in the pre-application stage, building on the start already made. The Trust also looks to be a more pro-active player in the church conservation field and would like to see itself distributing block grants on behalf of a Partnership of agencies who may well find that the Trust's economic administration and efficient monitoring capacity makes it a suitable vehicle for the redistribution of grant support.

The Trust has a strong network of professionals it can call upon to help in applications. I would like to thank these people for sharing their expert knowledge and skills with us and church congregations so that our ecclesiastical heritage can be better maintained for the future. This is a worthy and wonderful cause. The buildings we deal with, all across Scotland, represent a broad range of style and design, with small details sometimes hidden in a larger building that make you smile when you find them.

On behalf of the Trustees, I would also like to thank all those who have supported the Trust in the past, and hopefully on into the future. We are confident that the Scottish Churches Architectural Heritage Trust has the skills and administrative resources to ensure that the support we receive will be put to the very best of uses.

George W. Penrose,
Chairman.

SCOTTISH CHURCH HERITAGE RESEARCH

Volunteer House
69 Crossgate
Cupar
Fife KY15 5AS

Tel: 01334 844822. Email: schroffice@btconnect.com
Hon Secretary: John McQueen

Recently founded, the SCHR is a voluntary body comprising individuals from various faiths and professions. They share an interest in bringing to the public an understanding of all places and buildings used for worship in Scotland.

Volunteers are needed to:

- Record buildings
- Contribute information from publications and archives

They are at present assembling a gazetteer of Scottish places of worship. They publish a newsletter from time to time.

GLOSSARY

Apse	Semi-circular or polygonal end to a chancel as at Hoselaw Chapel, page 32.
Aumbry	Recess or cupboard, often lit up with an aumbry light, for sacred vessels.
Baldacchino	Free-standing canopy over an altar, originally made of fabric.
Barmkin	Wall enclosing courtyard attached to a tower house.
Box Pews	Wooden pews with surrounding sides for privacy and warmth. Some had their own fireplaces.
Bellcote	A bell-turret set on a roof or usually a gable. Birdcage bellcotes have frames around the bell. Often the rope is on the outside for the ringer (see Maxton Kirk, page 37).
Byzantine	In a Turkish or Byzantine style. See St Peter, Linlithgow (page 84).
But-and-Ben	Outer and inner rooms. Used as a description of a two-room cottage like that attached to Our Lady of the Snows, Tornahaish (page 25).
Clachan	A hamlet in Scotland.
Cleit	A stone storehouse. See St Kilda (page 79).
Crowsteps	Square stones set as steps, often in a gable end. See Our Lady of Perpetual Succour, Chapeltown (page 89).
Cutty Stool	Three-legged stool. See Symington, Ayrshire (page 30).

Dun	Small stone-walled fort. The hill on Iona is called Dun One.
Exedra	Another name for an apse.
Flèche or Spiret	A slim spire, often in the middle of a roof.
Forestair	Exterior stair, often leading to a gallery.
Gallery	Upper room above the aisle of a church, sometimes for the local squire or for musicians and often with a forestair.
Guild of Margarets	A society of ladies, all named Margaret, who look after St Margaret's Chapel, Edinburgh, especially the flowers.
Harl	A rough, hard-wearing plaster, particularly well-suited to protecting stonework from the Scottish climate.
Kingpost	Vertical timber set centrally on a tie-beam of a roof. See St Maelrubha, Poolewe (page 52).
Loft	Another name for a gallery. A trade's loft in a town was for the local tradesmen.
Luckenbooth	A lock-up booth or shop.
Mort-safe	An iron frame over a grave to keep out body-snatchers. There is one in Moy Churchyard.
Narthex	Enclosed vestibule or covered porch at the entrance to a church.
Oculus	A circular opening, often just a decoration as at Maxton, Borders (page 37).
Piend Roof	A hipped roof as at Dairsie, Fife (see page 44).
Pleasance	Walled garden or close.
Quarries	Square or diamond panes of glass, or possibly tiles or floor slabs.

Rainwater Goods	Architect's term for drainpipes and other water-carrying features.
Parliamentary Church	See section on Thomas Telford (page 77).
Sacristy	Room in a church for sacred vessels and vestments.
Sessions Clerk	Church of Scotland official, usually in charge of several churches. Keeps keys and can often take services.
Session House	Room or separate building for meetings of elders or ministers who form a kirk session.
Steading	A farm building or buildings. See Legerwood, Borders (page 34).
Tolbooth	A tax office containing council chamber and prison. See Legerwood, Borders (page 34).
Tron	A public weighing beam.
Wheel Window	A circular window with radiating shafts like spokes.
Yett	A metal-hinged gate made of iron bars alternately penetrating and penetrated. See Kisimul Castle (page 65).

BIBLIOGRAPHY

Burleigh, J.H.S., *A Church History of Scotland*, Oxford 1960

Scotland Churches Scheme, *1000 Churches to Visit in Scotland*, Edinburgh 2003 & 2005

Bone, S., *West Coast Skye to Oban*, Shell Guide, London 1952

(Alas, what happened to the rest of the Scotland Shell Guides?)

Buchan, J., *The Kirk in Scotland 1560-1929*, Edinburgh 1930

Donnelly, M., *Scotland's Stained Glass*, Edinburgh 1997

Fenwick, H., *Scotland's Historic Buildings*, London 1974

Glendinning, M., MacInnes, R. and MacKechnie, A., *A History of Scottish Architecture*, Edinburgh 1996

Haswell-Smith, H., *The Scottish Islands*, Canongate, Edinburgh 2004

Howat, A.J. and Seton, M., *Churches of Moray*, Elgin 1981

Marwick, H., *Orkney*, London 1951

Matthesen & Ors, *The Outer Hebrides Handbook*, Machynlleth 1995

Munro, Sinclair and Ors, *Scottish Island Hopping*, Edinburgh 1992

Murphy, A., *Scotland's Highlands and Islands*, Bath 2007

Murray, G. and Wolfe, Capt., *The Tweeddale Shooting Club – a Memoir*, Edinburgh 1946

Seton, G., *Highways and Byways in the West Highlands*, London 1935

Seton, G., *Highlands of Scotland*, London 1951

Tait, C., *The Shetland Guide Book*, Orkney 1998

Williamson, K., *Fair Isle and Its Birds*, Edinburgh 1965

Pevsner Guides

Cruft, Dunbar & Fawcett, *Borders*, London 2006

Gifford, J., *Dumfries and Galloway*, London 1996

Gifford, J., *Highlands and Islands*, London 1992

Gifford, J., *Perth and Kinross*, London 2007

Gifford and McWilliam, *Edinburgh*, London 1984

McWilliam, *Lothian*, London 1978

Walker, F.A., *Argyll & Bute*, London 2000

Walker & Wilson, *Fife*, London 1988

Walker, Gifford and Stirling, *Central Scotland*, London 2002

Magazines, Journals and Articles

Inspires magazine, produced by SEC Edinburgh
Scottish Field
Deeside Field

Article by Mhairi Ross:
'A Jewel in the West – The Little Church at Ballachulish', July 2009
Scottish Field

Article by Alisdair Roberts:
'The Chapel at Tornahaish', 20, 1989
Deeside Field

INDEX

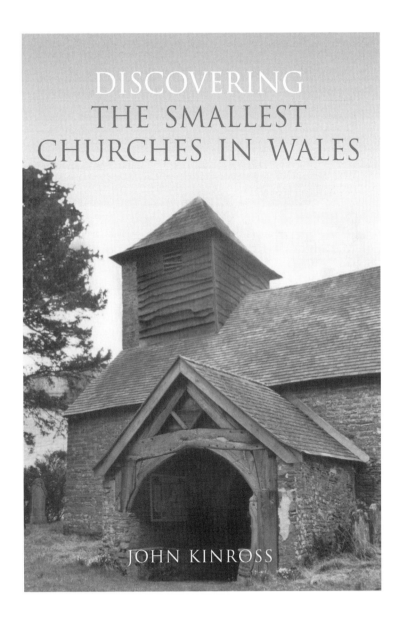

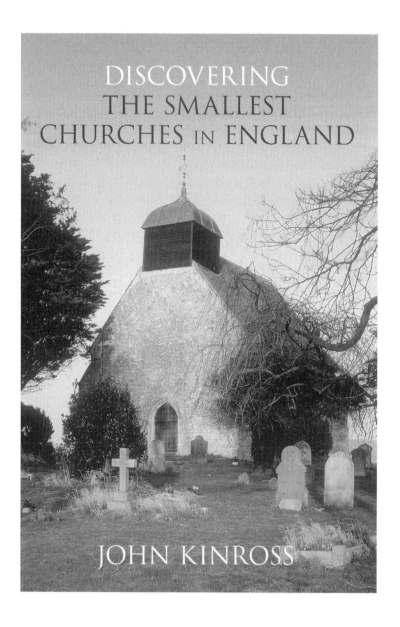

Discovering the Smallest Churches in England

by John Kinross

£16.99

978 0 7524 4779 6

THE HISTORY PRESS

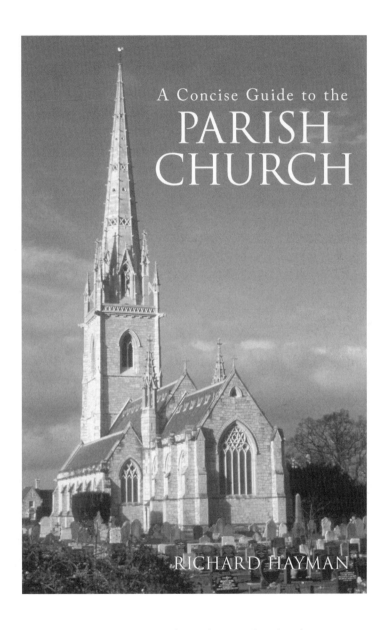

A Concise Guide to the Parish Church
by Richard Hayman
£15.99
978 0 7524 4095 8

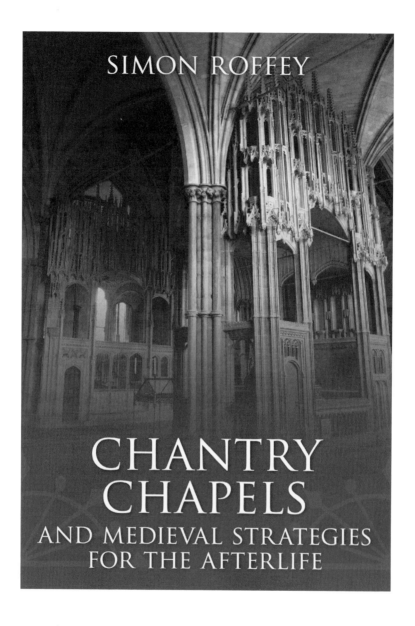

SIMON ROFFEY

CHANTRY
CHAPELS
AND MEDIEVAL STRATEGIES
FOR THE AFTERLIFE

Chantry Chapels and Medieval Strategies for the Afterlife
by Simon Roffey
£17.99
978 0 7524 4571 7